Moral Infringement and Repair in Antiquity

Supplement 2: *Group Dynamics*

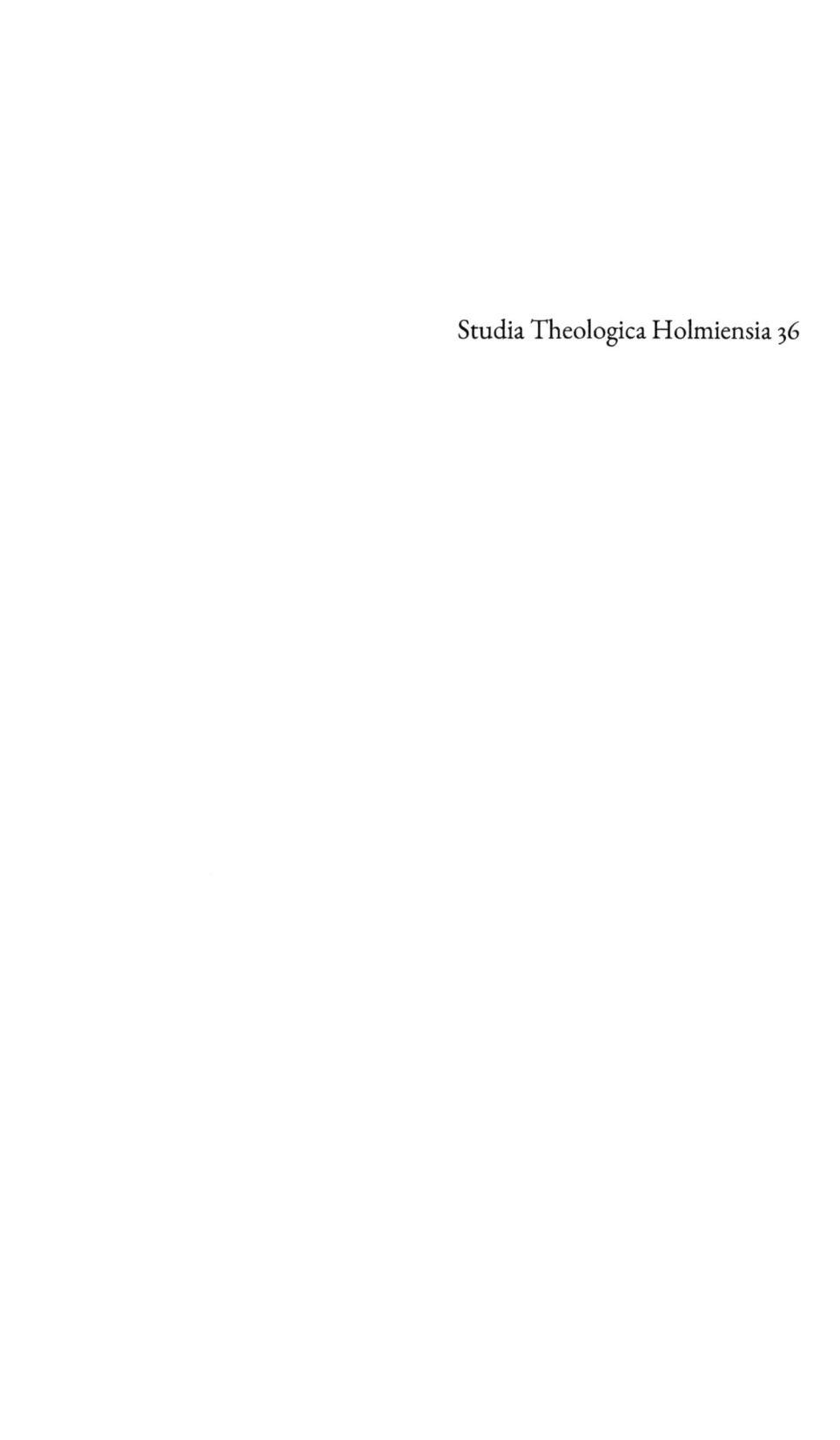
Studia Theologica Holmiensia 36

Rikard Roitto

Moral Infringement and Repair in Antiquity

Supplement 2:
Group Dynamics

Enskilda Högskolan Stockholm
2022

ISBN: 978-91-88906-19-9

Cover design: Carl Johan Berglund.
Cover images: Fragments of Roman wall painting (first century CE).
Metropolitan Museum of Art. Public domain.
Typeset in EB Garamond.
Printed by BoD – Books on Demand, Norderstedt, Germany.

Enskilda Högskolan Stockholm
Åkeshovsvägen 29, 168 39 Bromma
www.ehs.se

Preface

The present volume presents results from the project "Dynamics of Moral Repair in Antiquity," funded by the Swedish Research Council, grant nr. 2016-02319, between 2017 and 2021. The main publication, *Interpersonal Infringement and Moral Repair: Revenge, Compensation and Forgiveness in the Ancient World* is forthcoming in 2023 with Mohr Siebeck, in the WUNT series.

However, during the course of the project we have also produced a number of journal articles and book chapters. Most of these are now being collected and republished by EHS (Enskilda Högskolan Stockholm = University College Stockholm) in a number of supplementary volumes, which will be available both in print and freely online (ehs.se/moralrepair).

Supplement 2: *Group Dynamics*, contains four articles and chapters by Rikard Roitto. They are republished in accordance with the publishers' general conditions for author reuse, or by special permission, with minor corrections. The sources are as follows:

"Rituals of Reintegration," in *Oxford Handbook of Early Christian Ritual* (ed. Risto Uro, Richard E. DeMaris, Juliette J. Day, and Rikard Roitto; Oxford: Oxford University Pres, 2018), 426–443.

"Reintegrative Shaming and a Prayer Ritual of Reintegration in Matthew 18:15–20," *Svensk Exegetisk Årsbok* 97 (2014): 95–123.

"Enduring Shame as Costly Signalling: The Case of Public Confession of Sin According to Tertullian," *Journal of Cognitive Historiography* 4 (2017):60–78.

"The Johannine Information War: A Social Network Analysis of the Information Flow between Johannine Assemblies as Witnessed by 1–3 John," in *Drawing and Transcending Boundaries in the New Testament and Early Christianity* (ed. Jacobus Kok, Martin Webber, and Jermo van Nes; Berlin: LIT Verlag, 2019), 69–84.

Stockholm School of Theology, Bromma, June 2022
Thomas Kazen & Rikard Roitto

Contents

Rituals of Reintegration

Penance, Confession of Sins, Intercession

Introduction

In early Christianity, conflict resolution that involved decisions about exclusion and reintegration of community members was often ritualized as excommunication, penance, confession of sins, and intercession. Mediation of divine forgiveness of sin was central to the rituals that reintegrated transgressing community members and reconciled them with the community. How did these early Christians experience the ritual forgiveness of sins? How could the shame of penance and confession function in a reintegrative manner? How did confession function as costly signalling of commitment? In what way did confession and intercession function to maintain social identity?

Several excellent histories of the emergence of penance in the first centuries of Christianity have already been written (Favazza 1988; Goldhahn-Müller 1989; Fitzgerald 2008). The present discussion, in contrast, progresses thematically and discusses different types of ritualized reintegration, exemplified in important early Christian texts (1st to 3rd centuries).

The Experience of Ritual Forgiveness of Sins

In early Christianity immoral behaviour was conceived of as sin, which was a danger to both the individual and the community. Reintegration to the church was understood as removal of sin. Therefore, our study of ritualized reintegration begins with an appreciation of the experienced danger of sin and the experienced ritual efficacy of intercession for forgiveness in early Christianity.

The Danger of Sin

With the aid of conceptual metaphor theory (Lakoff and Johnson 1980; 1999), recent scholarship on the Jewish and Christian concept of sin has demonstrated that
sin was not just an abstract moral concept but rather spoken of as something quite
tangible. Gary Anderson (2009), discussing both Judaism and Christianity, shows
that in pre-exilic times sin was typically talked about as a substance, either a burden
or a stain, that needed to be removed from the sinner (e.g., Gen 4:13; Ps 51:4). After
the Babylonian exile, a second and complementary conceptualization of sin
emerged: sin as debt that needs to be forgiven and compensated for through good
deeds or suffering (e.g., Isa 40:2; Sir 3:3). Joseph Lam (2016) refines Anderson's
analysis of the Hebrew Bible and suggests four conceptualizations of sin: sin as
burden, accounting, path (e.g., Ps 119:101), and stain. To be complete, we should
add Paul's innovative conceptualization of sin as an agent, a slave-owner, in Ro-
mans 5–8.

  In all these conceptualizations, sin is something dangerous that destroys the
sinner's life and relationship to God. The burden of sin wears the sinner down and
causes sickness; the stain of sin makes the sinner morally impure and thus abomi-
nable to God; the account of sin and good deeds makes the sinner liable to the
accountant and judge, that is, God; the path of sin leads the sinner astray; and the
slave-owner Sin is an irresistible commanding force who makes the sinner break
God's law, which ultimately leads to death. The effect of sin is therefore experienced as dangerous, not just because it threatens interpersonal relationships, but
also because it threatens one's life and standing before God.

The Ritual Removal of Sin

A number of New Testament texts give us glimpses of early Christian rituals that
effect forgiveness of sins through intercession for sinners in the Christian community. (The extent to which baptism and the Eucharist were imagined to effect forgiveness is not dealt with in this chapter.) The Epistle of James, for example, portrays sin as a destructive force that gives birth to death (1:15; cf. 5:20), a measure that
can be forgiven (5:15) and a substance that can be covered (5:20). James promises
that communal prayers by the elders accompanied by anointment and laying on
of hands can effect both forgiveness and healing, since righteous prayers are "powerful" and "effective" (5:14–15). Sin is thus parallel to sickness in the sense that it is
a destructive force that threatens life but can be removed by prayer, anointing, and
laying on of hands on the sinner. The claim is backed with the example of Elijah

(5:16–17), which suggests that the author imagines the power of God to work through the prayers of the intercessors to take away the danger of sin.

According to the ritual form hypothesis (McCauley and Lawson 2002), the human mind structures its perception of religious ritual action in the same manner it structures ordinary actions, with the addition that divine agency somehow acts through the ritual action. Our cognitive schema for an ordinary action is that a) an agent performs an b) action (with an instrument) c) on a patient. In religious rituals God acts through one of these slots. God acts either through either a) the ritual agent (e.g., the priest), b) the ritual action and medium (e.g., words, gestures, or props), or even c) directly on the ritual patient (e.g., the penitent or the baptizand) to effect change of religious significance. Rituals of forgiveness of sins are perceived as rituals in which God somehow works through the ritual actions to take away the sin from the sinner. In the Epistle of James, the divine agency works through the intercessors (the ritual agents) and the laying on of hands and the anointments (the ritual instruments) to effect the removal of sin in the confessor (ritual patient). Similar practices are evident in the Matthean (Matt. 18:15–20) and the Johannine (John 20:22–23; 1 John 1:8–2:2; 5:14–18) traditions (Roitto 2012; 2014).

From the third century and onwards several texts deal with penance and intercessory prayers for sinners in greater depth (Favazza 1988: chs. 3–4). The urgent sense of sin as danger is even more apparent in many of these texts. When Tertullian wishes to convince his audience how important it is to do penance for postbaptismal sin in his treatise *On Repentance*, he talks about sin as a debt that must be repaid to avoid death (chs. 2–3), a shipwreck from which the only salvation is the plank of penance (chs. 4, 7), an offence to God that makes the sinner displeasing in God's eyes (ch. 5), a shameful and lethal venereal disease (ch. 10), etc. To remedy this state, the sinner must first do penance to honour God. Tertullian's imagination of an offended God that must be appeased fits well into David Konstan's (2010) analysis of ancient conflict resolution, where the most important part of moral repair was to restore the dignity of the offended party. In cases where the offender is clearly subordinate to the offended, this was best done by displays of submissiveness and shame (2010: 22–26, 59). As Tertullian imagines sin, the subordinate human had offended the superior God. Rough clothing, fasting, and weeping, as prescribed by Tertullian in *On Repentance*, ritualizes the acknowledgement of one's guilt and the appeasement of God (Ch. 9, 11). The penance ritual is concluded by public confession of sins (*exomologesis*), kneeling before the community (Ch. 9), and the laying of hands by the clergy (cf. *De Pud.* 7). This ritual finalizes the process that relieves the sinner from the danger of sin. The community represents Christ's agency (*De Paen.* 10) and therefore the ritual "exalts" (*relevat*), "cleanses" (*mundatum reddit*), "excuses" (*excusat*) and "absolves" (*absolvit*) the penitent from sin (Ch. 9).

Cyprian's argument in his treatise *On the Lapsed* is basically very similar to Tertullian's: It is dangerous to avoid penance and confession of sins since it will lead to damnation. Cyprian conveys an even more acute sense of danger when he reiterates colourful example stories about unrepentant sinners who were tormented and killed by demons, made dumb, vomited after partaking in the Eucharist, and so on (chs. 24–26). Only sincere penance can remedy the dire state you are in.

To sum up the argument of this section, sin was perceived as a concrete danger by the first Christians and the rituals of penance, confession, and intercession were experienced as its remedy. In terms of ritual theory, specifically Jens Schjødt's (1986) classification of rituals, we can classify these rituals as crisis rituals, that is, rituals that take the ritual patient from a negative to a normalized state. Crisis rituals can be contrasted with rites of passage, which take the patient form one neutral status to another within the community, and rites of initiation, which transforms the patient from an outsider to an insider. The sinner was neither an acceptable community member, nor an outsider, but a deviant in danger who needed to be restored.

The Costliness of Post-Baptismal Forgiveness

Why did the early church not just forgive the sins of postbaptismal sinners without discrimination? Given our discussion in the previous section about sin as life-threatening danger, it would seem uncontroversial for the church to use its authority to redeem everyone without limitation in order to save them. From an emic theological perspective, restrictions on forgiveness were explained with images like that of Tertullian's anthropomorphic God who is angered by sin and will not forgive until he has been appeased by sincere remorse. Thus, rituals of forgiveness could never be a mechanical way to bypass God's indignation over immorality. Just like interpersonal apologies are experienced as more sincere if they are accompanied by costly gestures (Ohtsubo and Watanabe 2008), so was God experienced as more pleased by thorough penance practices. From an etic perspective, though, explanations based on God's anthropomorphic character traits are insufficient. We also need to discuss the social effects of costly reconciliatory rituals in early Christian communities.

Game Theory and the Limits of Post-Baptismal Forgiveness

Reconciliation is the beginning of renewed cooperation, and cooperation is one of humanity's most fundamental dilemmas. Should I cooperate only with fully reliable partners, or should I accept cooperation with even the nastiest cheats who will probably take advantage of me at every opportunity? Or should I try to find a strategy somewhere in between? What is the most optimal strategy? Game theory is a theoretical discipline that analyses problems of cooperation and competition between social agents with the aid of mathematical models and computer simulations of agents. One of the pioneers of the field, Robert Axelrod (1984; 1997), made several computer simulations of social agents that need to cooperate repeatedly to gain resources and thus be able to reproduce. The artificial agents in these simulations are simpleminded compared to humans, but nevertheless employ basic strategies to decide whether they should continue to cooperate with other agents in the next round or not. In these simulations, an agent can receive extra resources by defecting from cooperation and taking advantage of a cooperative agent, but if both agents defect in the same round, both end up with nothing at all. In several versions of Axelrod's simulations, agents can cooperate, be "nasty" (defect to gain an advantage) or "take revenge" (defect as soon as the other agent has defected). Cooperative agents can also "forgive" defectors, which means that the agent continues to cooperate in the next round even if the other agent defects. Axelrod was able to show that limited forgiveness (continue to cooperate with a defector once or twice before you take revenge) is a more successful strategy than both nastiness (always defect), tit-for-tat (take revenge immediately) and relentless forgiveness (always cooperate) under many circumstances, especially in circumstances where the simulated agents are programmed to make "mistakes" (defect when their strategy says cooperate and vice versa) at random intervals. If an agent never forgives even the smallest slight, that agent will end up losing valuable partners who made mistakes, but if the agent forgives unceasingly, the agent will end up robbed of all resources, exploited by nasty agents. To forgive defectors one or two times but not more than that was an optimal middle road to avoid losing cooperative partners who make occasional mistakes and yet protect oneself from habitual defectors.

Research involving simulations of social behaviour has proliferated, resulting in innumerable tests of various cooperation scenarios. For our purposes, however, the pioneering simulations by Axelrod are enough to demonstrate that every individual and every group have to make calculated decisions on a daily basis about whom to cooperate with. We humans are intuitive game theoreticians (some more skilled than others) who consciously or subconsciously weigh the costs and benefits of cooperating or not cooperating with people around us. Psychologists and biologists argue that the emotional set-up to balance forgiveness and revenge is innate in both humans and other social species (McCullough 2008). We may therefore assume that the first Christian groups were just like us in this sense.

The problem of forgiveness is evident already in the tension between different sayings of Jesus on the subject. Several sayings radically demand unlimited forgiveness, reconciliation, and non-retaliation (Mark 11:25; Matt 5:38–48; 6:9, 14–15; 18:21–35; Luke 6:29–36; 11:4), while other sayings limit the duty to forgive offenders to those who "repent" or "listen" (Luke 17:3–4; Matt 18:15–22). The latter sayings deal with forgiveness of "brothers" meant to function as intra-group ethics for Christian communities, which might explain why the ethics of forgiveness is conditional in these sayings. We may imagine that early Christian communities, just like any community, made the intuitive strategic judgment call that they had to limit forgiveness of repeat offenders in their community.

If early Christian communities worked anything like most social groups, most interpersonal conflicts were probably solved in a non-ritualized manner. In Paul's letter we find all kinds of conflicts, such as interpersonal conflicts (e.g., Phil. 4:2–3), factions inside the communities (e.g., 1 Cor. 1–4), and conflicts between different branches of the Church (Galatians). In none of these cases does Paul call for ritualized protocols for conflict resolution. On one occasion, however, we see a glimpse of ritualization of conflict resolution (DeMaris 2008: 79–90): Paul argues that that they should "hand" a sexual offender "over to Satan for the destruction of the flesh" (1 Cor. 5:5), which is probably a curse formula (Smith 2009). (The *anathema* curses pronounced by Paul, Gal 1:8–9; 1 Cor 16:22, are not directed at individuals but rather against anyone who holds certain opinions and can therefore not be seen as rituals of exclusion.)

The sexual offender is the only known case where Paul suggests exclusion or marginalization (we do not know which, but Pauls specifies that they should not eat together, 1 Cor. 5:11) of a community member, and it is in this particular case where we see some degree of ritualization of the conflict resolution. To hand the sinner over to Satan is a way to ritualize the individual's change of status. According to Roy Rappaport (1999: e.g., 89–97), rituals function to make the new status of individuals an unambiguous social fact. Throughout the early history of the church, conflicts involving decisions about exclusion and reintegration are more ritualized than other conflicts. (More on this below.)

Why would Paul exclude this particular member, when he seems to think that the whole Corinthian community is full of sinful behaviour? His argument is that this particular sin is like "leaven" (1 Cor 5:6–10) that will destroy the whole community, and thus frames the problem in terms of the purity of the church (De-Maris 2008:79–90). The imagery suggests that Paul has made an intuitive game theoretical calculus and come to the conclusion that this particular individual's defection from group norms is going to have particularly contagious consequences for the moral purity of the whole community. In other words, Paul seems worried about the integrity of the social identity of the community if they allow the moral transgressor to participate in their meals. Whether Paul is strategically correct in his decision is not our issue here. For our discussion, the important point is that Paul's theological reasoning embeds intuitive strategic judgment calls.

Matthew 18:15–20 contains the New Testament's most developed script for conflict resolution. Yet it is somewhat unrealistic in the sense that it assumes one sinner and one victim, and since it assumes that the victim has the courage to confront the abuser alone, which is rarely the case in real life conflicts. The Matthean Jesus prescribes a three-step procedure to put increasing pressure on the offender to "listen," and if he does not listen, he is to be excluded or marginalized (vv. 15–17). The three verses that follow (vv. 18–20) seem to reflect a ritual pronouncement in the community where the sinner is either "bound" or "loosened" depending on whether he listens (Roitto 2014). The whole procedure is geared toward exclusion as a very last resort, and the emphasis in chapter 18 lies on forgiveness and efforts to reform the offender. The Matthean script of conflict resolution embeds the game-theoretical insight that it is often a good idea to continue to cooperate with occasional offenders, but that one should stop cooperating with those who do not recognize their offence as morally wrong, since they will likely repeat their offence.

To what extent the Christian community should continue to tolerate repeated offenders is at the core of the debate in the following centuries about whether one should allow forgiveness of grave sins after baptism. In the east, unlimited forgiveness of repeated offences as long as the sinner repented was the norm, but in Rome and Northern Africa, a debate on this issue raged in the second and third century (Favazza 1988: chs. 2–4). The Shepherd of Hermas is the first Christian author to suggest one more – but only one – chance to be forgiven after baptism (Herm. Vis. 2.2.4–5; Herm. Mand. 4.1.8; 4.3.6).

Tertullian, known for his rigorist bent, also argues for limiting the post-baptismal penance to one occasion in *On Repentance* (ch. 7), written before he joined the Montanists. Later in life, after becoming a Montanist, he argues in *On Modesty* that certain sins, especially adultery, can never be forgiven. He makes a distinction between sins "unto death," which cannot be forgiven, and less grave sins "not unto death," which can be forgiven repeatedly (ch. 2). With this new distinction, he abandons the category of sins that can be forgiven once. He does so in debate with an unnamed bishop, who apparently has decreed that all adulterers will be forgiven if they repent (ch. 1). To Tertullian, this is to destroy any incitement to stop sinning, since the sinner knows in advance that his sin will not endanger his salvation. The lenient attitude of the bishop will only increase sin in the church, Tertullian argues (ch. 1).

Tertullian and Hermas could be said to formulate game strategies when they formulate rules for how many times and how gravely people may sin before they are no longer allowed to be part of the community. The rule of one second penance is similar to the strategy "forgiving tit-for-tat," which proved to be quite successful in Axelrod's simulations. This strategy forgives cooperation partners once in order to not terminate cooperation too fast, but after that one should deny further cooperation to avoid further damage. Since Hermas is motivated by a sense of eschatological urgency, this solution might seem game-theoretically sound. One more chance should be enough if the final judgment is around the corner. However, history proved Hermas wrong in his eschatological expectation, which made the rule of only one second penance quite impractical since it was too inflexible to cover the complexities of long-term collaboration. In Northern Africa and Rome, there was intense debate in the third century between rigorists, laxists and those in between about how generously the Church should forgive post-baptismal sinners (Dallen 1986: ch. 2; Favazza 1988: ch. 4). The debate climaxed in the aftermath of the Decian persecution. After much strife, the bishops in Northern Africa accepted Cyprian's policy in *On the Lapsed* to reconcile everyone who made proper penance, but those who had actually sacrificed to idols had to make lifelong penance. However, just two years later, 252 CE, it was decided that even those who had sacrificed should be fully reconciled with the church (Dallen 1986: 38–39).

The history of regulating excommunication, penance and reconciliation in the early Church is thus the history of trying to formulate what we from an etic, game-theoretical, perspective can describe as a functional balance between exclusion and inclusion that could maintain the integrity of the Church. Determining the appropriate balance depends on what kind of church you wish to uphold, and had we moved later in history, we would have seen that the experimentation on rules for church discipline is a never-ending struggle (Dallen 1986). Rigorists like Tertullian envisioned a holy community of highly committed and moral members. Cyprian's vision for the church was obviously more tolerant of shortcomings. Different understandings of the identity of the church obviously led to different intuitions about a good balance between reintegration and permanent exclusion. From the perspective of cultural epidemiology (Sperber 1996) congregations that practiced the policy to reintegrate all who were willing to do penance were probably capable of creating more vital communities than both rigorists and laxists in the long run. The rigorist's policy probably excluded too many members and thus was not capable of dispersing effectively in the population of the Roman Empire. At first glance, one might think that a laxist policy would have had the best potential to spread across a population, since it is the most inclusive policy. However, as we will develop further in the sections below with the help of costly signalling theory, the laxist position probably made the identity of the church less distinct and inspired lower degrees of commitment to the extent that laxist congregations were not as stable as those churches that required penance.

Penance and Public Confession of Sins as Costly Signalling

In recent debates about the evolutionary roots of religion, one of the most fundamental research debates is whether religion is best explained as the by-product of functional cognition or as an adaptation that enhances cooperation. Proponents of the adaptationist theory have suggested that religious rituals can function as costly signals of commitment (Irons 1996, 2001; Sosis 2003, 2004, 2006). A commitment signal is an action – often a ritual action – to prove one's commitment to the community. The action must be difficult to fake and so costly that it is only worthwhile if you are committed to the group. Less committed persons would find the cost of such a ritual too high to participate. In early Christianity baptism gradually developed into a costly signal of commitment as the catechumenate became longer and more demanding and as the baptismal ritual became more elaborate (cf. Johnson 2007). Only a fairly committed person would make the effort to go through all the stages necessary to become a full member of the church in the third and fourth centuries.

Nevertheless, even church members who were committed enough at the time of baptism were perhaps not always motivated to abide by the norms of the Christian community. How was one to determine whether such a member should remain in the community? I suggest that public confession of sins and penance functioned as a costly signal of commitment in the early Church.

The Shame of Public Confession as a Costly Signal

The cost of a ritual can be quite material, such as sacrifice of animals or mutilation of the body. But the cost can also be immaterial, such as time, risking social status, giving up social relations, or emotional stress. I suggest here that risking shame was the cost of public confession of sins.

Irenaeus (*Adv. Haer.* I.13.7) mentions that some are ashamed to confess their sins and therefore apostatize. Shame is also recognized by Tertullian as the main obstacle to overcome in his discussion in *On Repentance*. He realizes that some hesitate to confess their sins because they "anticipate shame" (ch. 10), but argues that the shame is worth it, because salvation is at stake.

Psychologists describe shame as an emotion that makes you feel unworthy in the face of others, as opposed to the feeling of guilt, which makes you feel negatively about certain acts you have committed (e.g., Tangney 2002; Tangney and Dearing 2002). Anthropologists, on the other hand, often talk about shame as the opposite of honour. Whereas honour is positive social capital, shame is negative social capital (e.g., Peristiany 1966; Gilmore 1987; Rohrbaugh 2010). There is, of course, a connection between the emotional and social aspect since social shame often causes the emotional state of shame. Carlin Barton argues that ancient Roman discourse on shame distinguished between the sense of shame, that is, an inner sensitivity to what is shameful, and actual shame, that is, losing honour in the face of others. Displaying the emotion shame could sometimes lessen the social shame, since the display demonstrated a sense of shame (Barton 2001: 197–296).

From an evolutionary perspective, the emotion shame increases fitness by inhibiting certain behaviours that would potentially disqualify us from the goods that having cooperation partners brings (Gilbert 2003; cf. Jaffe 2008). Like all emotions, shame is sometimes a crude instrument that can misfire or become pathological. Evolutionary psychologists recognize this but argue that shame on average guides social behaviour in directions that increase fitness. The capacity to anticipate what will cause shame is as important as the actual experience of shame, since our anticipation inhibits our behaviour before we have done something anti-social (Greenwald and Harder 1998).

Shame can induce several different courses of action (Gilbert 2003; Greenwald and Harder 1998; Tangney and Dearing 2002). When someone feels shame for breaking social norms, it often induces an impulse to repair relations by showing submissiveness. However, shame can also provoke an impulse to hide from the shaming gaze of the group. Shame can therefore both induce pro-social and anti-social behaviour. (Another domain of shame is related to competition for social status. When you have been shamed and denigrated in a contest for social honour, the most typical reactions are mortification, anger, desire for revenge, and longing to regain your honour. However, that is not our focus here.)

Societies often use processes of shaming to rear their members and direct behaviour. Criminologist John Braithwaite (1989) helpfully distinguishes between stigmatizing and reintegrative shaming. When shaming is stigmatizing, the processes push the offender out of societal acceptance so that the offender distances himself from the group. When shaming is reintegrative, it is coupled with love and hope of forgiveness. The offender is put to shame, but also welcomed back to the group and accepted anew as soon as the offender shows willingness to reform and atone for his/her crime. Reintegrative shaming as a strategy to reform offenders only works if the offender values his/her belonging to the shaming community. The period of shaming must be limited, and the intensity of the shame must not be too overwhelming, Braithwaite argues. Forceful shaming strategies often result in stigmatization.

Given the nature of shame, public confession of sins was probably an effective commitment signal. A good costly signal should deter the uncommitted more than the committed, and shame can function to either alienate or to reintegrate community members. Tertullian is well aware that the emotional and social shame of public confession is experienced as such a high cost that some hesitate to confess in spite of its leading to eternal life. Therefore, Tertullian comforts those who hesitate to confess that they will be met by loving care by the community, since the other community members are so socially close that they could not possibly take advantage of the precarious situation of the confessor:

> If ever the danger to shame is serious, this is certainly the case when it stands in the presence of insult and mockery, when one man is exalted through another's ruin, when one ascends over another who is laid low. But among brethren and fellow-servants, where there is one hope, fear, joy, sorrow, suffering, because there is one Spirit from one Lord and Father, why do you think these men are any[thing] different from yourself (lat. *hos aliud quam te opinaris*)? Why do you flee, as of scoffers, those who share your misfortunes? The body cannot rejoice at the suffering of a single of its members; the whole body must needs suffer along with it and help in its cure. (*Paen.* 10, transl. Le Saint 1959; cf. *Pud.* 3)

Tertullian's scene is an excellent example of what Braithwaite calls 'reintegrative shaming'. The confessor can feel the care from the community as he confesses and becomes reintegrated into the community again. To those strongly committed, the shaming ritual of confession was probably experienced as limited suffering worth enduring to be reconciled with the community and removed from one's former status as sinner.

A less committed member, however, might have felt less confidence in the loving goodness of the 'brothers' and reckoned the value of reintegration lower – the risks of his confession being used against him as costlier than the benefit of being allowed to return to the community – even if one believed in Christ as one's saviour.

As discussed above, shame can both give the impulse to reconcile through submissive displays and the impulse to withdraw, depending on how important the relation is. Therefore confession functioned as a costly signal that deterred the less committed but reintegrated the committed. The cost-benefit-analysis of the individual contemplating whether to confess or not would have led to different estimates depending on the degree of commitment. By exploiting the human action impulses associated with shame, penance effectively induced different choices, depending on commitment.

In the first and second century texts that talk about reproof, confession, and intercession there is no explicit mention of a period of ascetic penance preceding the public confession. However, in the third century several texts give witness to how the church developed different kinds of ascetic penance practices. Tertullian is a vivid witness to a practice in which the penitent goes through a period of simple clothing and food accompanied by prayers and tears (*Paen.* 9–11). Tertullian has often been interpreted as a legalist who thinks one can compensate for sins by penitential merits. Gösta Hallonsten (1982) has argued, however, that Tertullian's language should not be mistaken for legalism. Rather than legal satisfaction, Tertullian demands gestures of good will towards God. In the analytical language of costly signalling theory, Tertullian compels Christians to send a costly signal of commitment to God and to the community.

The severity of Tertullian's prescriptions brings us to the problem of balanced costly signalling. According to costly signalling theory, it is not the case that a more costly ritual practice always is better. On the contrary, overly costly rituals will repel even committed community members. A functional costly signalling ritual should not be so costly that it deters more cooperation partners than necessary (Sosis 2003). Apparently, the unnamed bishop who Tertullian opposes in *On Modesty* as well as many others in Tertullian's church made different judgment calls as to how severe and restricted penance should be. A few decades later, after the Decian persecution, rigorists called for severe penance and even permanent exclusion of the lapsed while the laxists allowed anyone who repented to return without penance. Cyprian argued for a middle road (see discussion above). This shows how difficult it was to steer penance in a direction that on the one hand was costly enough to deter less committed opportunists, but on the other hand not so severe that it repelled highly committed believers.

Matthew 18:15–20 appears to be an early attempt at softening the amount of shame involved in reproof of sinners (Roitto 2014). Many other instructions from the first century simply prescribe that sinners should be isolated from the Christian community if they do not listen to reproof (e.g., 1 Cor 5:9–11; 2 Thess 3:14; Tit 3:10; *Did.* 15:3), but Matthew prescribes an approach whereby the sinner should preferably just be reproved by a small group and only as a last resort by the whole community. According to Braithwaite's analysis of reintegrative shaming, reintegration works best if the amount of shame is moderate and combined with care and love for the transgressor, so we may suspect that Matthew reacted against dysfunctional reproof practices in his community that pushed away people that could otherwise have been reintegrated. The church experimented a lot with the degree of publicity in the process of penance during the first six centuries, but in the 7th century the practice was radically reformed so that confession of sin was with very few exceptions a non-public ritual before a priest rather than the congregation (Rahner 1983: e.g., 216–217; McNeill and Gamer 1938:3–75).

When the costly rituals prescribed by the leadership are experienced as too tough, community members might be inclined to find workarounds. As William Irons (2001), one of the pioneers of costly signalling theory, points out, costly rituals can usually only be upheld if the leadership can enforce them. In early Christianity, the belief that martyrs had the authority to forgive sins became popular in the third century. Asking a martyr for intercession thus became a way to bypass penance. Already Tertullian protests against this innovation (*Pud.* 22), but it is during the Decian persecution that the practice becomes most popular. Instead of going through penance, some would ask a soon-to-be martyr for a letter of indulgence to show that one's sins had been atoned through the powerful intercession of the martyr. In practice, this belief undermined the bishop's control of the penitential process and thereby also of who was allowed back into the community. Not surprisingly, Cyprian argued against the practice of bypassing proper penance with indulgences (*Laps.* 17; *Ep.* 29, 30; cf. Dallen 1986: 37–42), even if he did not deny the efficacy of the martyrs' intercessions (*Ep.* 8; *Laps.* 36).

Public Confession and Excommunication as Identity Maintenance

Being a Christian in the early church was obviously not just a matter of belonging to a functional group that could cooperate to produce material welfare. The identity of the Christian community was that it was a community with shared beliefs, norms, and goals. Rituals of exclusion and reintegration were therefore tools for maintaining the identity of the church.

Reintegration as Identity Maintenance

Roy Rappaport (1999:52–54) suggests that rituals elicit two kinds of information that are important for the community: self-referential information and canonical information. Self-referential information is the information that the participants of a ritual elicit about themselves by participating in the ritual. In the case of public confession of sins, the confessor sends the information that he repents his sin, accepts the values of the group, and intends to live by them from now on. The publicity of the act, where the sinner kneels and weeps and receives intercession (Tertullian, *Paen.* 9–10), makes the sinner's detachment from sin and commitment to his/her identity as a member of church a social fact. The confessor could theoretically fake sincerity, but as Rappaport (1999:119–124) points out, the ritual makes one's commitment a social fact and an obligation that can be held against whoever does not abide by it. The ritual thus increases the social pressure for the participant to be consistent with the self-referential information she/he has given in the ritual.

Canonical information is information about the worldview of the community. Whenever a penitent confesses sins publicly, he/she simultaneously confirms the values and the worldview of the church. *Didascalia Apostolorum* 11 reasons that the confession of one community member is really beneficial for the whole community, since if the rest of the community sees a sinner participating the communion, they might think it is acceptable to sin themselves. Cyprian argues in *On the Lapsed* that it would be a mockery of those who died for their convictions during the persecution to allow the lapsed to return to the church without proper penance and confession of sins. He praises how those who had the courage to confess their faith during the persecution. They embody the identity of the church, while the cowardice of the lapsed is contrary to all values of the church (chs. 1–13). It is therefore contrary to the Gospel and a pollution of the church to allow the lapsed back without proper penance (chs. 14–16). Proper penance and confession, on the other hand, is good for the whole church (chs. 35–36). In both these texts, the authors are themselves aware of how penance and confession of sins publicly expresses the communal identity.

Exclusion as Identity Maintenance

Social psychologists frequently point out that shaming, marginalization, and exclusion of deviants can function to manifest the values for the whole group, even if the offender does not readjust. Josue Marques et al. (2001) call this "the black sheep effect." The sectarian writings of the Qumran literature, for example, contain rules for who is allowed to participate in the holy meals and how long one should be excluded from the meals depending on which group norms one has violated (1QS with parallels in D, e.g., 1QS VII, 18–25, see Jokiranta 2007). Jutta Jokiranta (2007) has argued convincingly that these rules contributed to preserving the identity of the community. It is reasonable to assume that the excommunication practices of the early church functioned in the same way. The manner of exclusion or marginalization varied considerably in the first centuries of the church, as Joseph Favazza has shown (1988). Some early texts advice that one should not even talk to excluded members, but as the penance system took shape, the most common practice was to bar the excommunicated member from participation in the Eucharist but still admonish the sinner to do penance. The latter is a form of marginalization rather than exclusion, with the goal of reintegrating the member. Common to both forms of excommunication, though, is the use of negative (black sheep) labelling to mark group boundaries and thus clarify the identity of the church.

Intercession for the Forgiveness of Sins in Egalitarian and Episcopal Churches

Lastly, a brief reflection on the different functions of intercession in egalitarian and hierarchical congregations. In the Gospel of Matthew and the Johannine texts, we find no hints of institutionalized and hierarchical leadership structures. On the contrary, the churches reflected in these texts seem comparatively egalitarian (Matt 20:25–28; 23:8–12; 1 John 2:20–21, 27). In these traditions, the authority to reprove and intercede for sinners is given to every "brother" (Matt 18:15–20; 1 John 5:14–17; Roitto 2012; 2014). On the other hand, James 5:14–15 appoints the authority to pray for sins and sickness to the elders and in the third century the authority to intercede for sins is firmly limited to the bishop and the elders (e.g., Tertullian, *Paen.* 9–10; *Didascalia* 52; 64–69; Cyprian, *Laps.* 29).

It is not very realistic to imagine that there were ever groups of Christ-devotees entirely lacking leadership structures (cf. Elliott 2002). Even in groups with egalitarian ideals, there are inevitably informal leaders. Nevertheless, in a few early Christian groups, the authority to intercede for the forgiveness of sin was apparently given to all community members. 1 John hints at a community in which everybody was encouraged to confess their sins in the community on a regular basis

(1 John 1:9) and each community member could intercede for sinning members (1 John 5:16; Roitto 2012). Matthew 18:15–20 seems to reflect a communal practice where all community members were authorized to reprove one another, and where small groups of community members, "two or three," were authorized to bind or lose the sinner (Roitto 2014).

In such communities, where each member had the power to relieve each other member from sin, we can imagine that the rituals of confession and intercession had cohesive effects for the community and helped with conflict resolution. Perspective-taking, where you have to think from the perspective of whoever you are in conflict with, is a well proven method for stimulating reconciliation between quarrelling individuals (e.g., Galinsky, Ku and Wang 2005; Takaku, Weiner and Ohbuchi 2001). Listening to confessions of sin and praying for the sinner made it necessary for the intercessor to take the perspective of the sinner. Mediating divine forgiveness allowed the mediator to take the perspective of God, and perhaps the imagination of a graceful God could inspire similar attitudes in the intercessor. We do not know whether the community member who was harmed by the sinner's wrongdoing was among those who interceded for the sinner, but if that was the case, the perspective-taking that the rituals stimulated would have been particularly effective for conflict resolution, since it is easier to forgive someone into whose shoes you have stepped. The scenario just painted is the product of an optimistic historical imagination, and it is equally easy to imagine how difficult it must have been to uphold such a system. Already 1 John 1:8 might suggest that some community members – understandably enough – preferred not to confess their sin publicly (cf. the discussion above on shame). The egalitarian version of reproof, confession of sins and intercession was probably difficult to uphold in the long run.

As opposed to the egalitarian version of confession and absolution, the hierarchically supported versions of these rituals were better equipped to handle the fact that people wished to avoid the shame of exposing their moral shortcomings. As discussed above in the section on costly signalling, costly rituals are much easier to impose if there are leadership structures that can enforce them. Penance governed by an institutionalized leadership, for better or worse, was thus a more powerful tool to maintain community borders and thus to preserve the leadership's vision for the identity of the church. The hierarchically governed version of penance, in turn, probably had a strengthening effect on the legitimacy of the leaders. The role of the bishop and the elders in *Didascalia Apostolorum*, for instance, intertwines the leaders' ritual functions with their general leadership roles. Among the bishop's duties is to judge and mediate in conflicts and decide on guilt and penance (ch. 10). The very same bishop is also the ritual agent of the rituals of excommunication and intercession after penance (ch. 7). If people perceived the bishop and the elders to have a unique authority to mediate forgiveness, then every performance of the ritual reinforced the perception of the leadership as sanctioned by God. This in turn, strengthened the legitimacy of the leaders to decide on resolutions to conflicts in the community.

Conclusion

Sin was experienced as a danger in early Christianity, and the identity of the church was the community of those saved from this danger and made holy through Jesus Christ. Rituals of penance and intercession were experienced as an effective remedy for the danger of postbaptismal sin. The ritualization of exclusion and reintegration also functioned to communicate status changes of individuals to the community. Those who were willing to do penance and confess their sins in the church sent a costly signal that ensured their commitment to the norms and the worldview of the church. As control over reproof, excommunication, penance, confession, and intercession was allotted to the bishop and the elders, these rituals also became important tools for communal border maintenance and manifestations of the identity of the church.

Acknowledgement: The research for this article was funded by the Finnish Research Council, grant nr. 1266452, and the Swedish Research Council, grant nr. 2016-02319.

Reintegrative Shaming and a Prayer Ritual of Reintegration in Matthew 18:15–20

Abstract

Matthew 18:15–20 promotes a practice of reproof and reintegration into the Matthean community. With the aid of John Braithwaite's reintegrative shaming theory, it is argued that Matthew aims to formulate a practice that combines shame and care in order to reintegrate offenders in the community. Moreover, ritual theories are used to argue that the promise of effective prayer in v. 19 reflects a reintegrative prayer ritual, which was experienced as effective in removing sin and signalled the reintegrated status of the sinning brother to the community.

An Initial Reading of Matt 18:15–20

The argument of this article is that Matt 18:15–20 aims to form a practice that can reintegrate offenders and manifest the offender's reintegration in a prayer ritual. By introducing reintegrative shaming theory and a number or ritual theories into the analysis, a deepened understanding of how the practices promoted in the passage might have worked in the Matthean community emerges. However, before we analyse Matthew 18:15–20 as a reintegrative practice, we need to establish that it is reasonable a) to read Matt 18:15–20 as a unit, b) to read the promises in vv. 18–20 as ritual instructions, c) to understand the prayer in v. 19 as the practical way to perform the binding and loosing mentioned in v. 18, and d) to interpret binding and loosing in v. 18 as mediating forgiveness of sin (that is, not just as making halakhic decisions).

Matt 18:15–20 has two distinguishable yet connected parts. The first part, vv. 15–17, instructs how to reprove a sinning brother. The goal is to make the sinning brother "listen," but if all efforts to talk to him fail, "he should be to you like a gentile and tax collector." The second part, vv. 18–20, consists of two promises on the theme that God will back up the community whatever they do, and a concluding assurance of presence among them. Whatever they "bind" or "loose" (v. 18), whatever they pray for (v. 19), God will make it happen.

At first glance, vv. 15–17 may look unrelated to vv. 18–20. However, recurring catchwords and sentence structures in the passage justifies thinking that Matthew intended it to be read as a literary unit, and thus that the prayer in 18:19 should be understood as connected to the reproof in 18:15–17. The passage is most probably composed from disparate traditions, but Matthew has clearly made an effort in his redaction to show that he thinks of the parts as connected (Thompson 1970: 175–202; Luz 2001: 448). First, the theme of "two or three" (vv. 16, 19, 20) connects vv. 15–17 with vv. 18–20. Second, all sentences but one (v. 20) in the passage have subordinate clauses beginning with *ean*, "if," or *hosa/hou ean*, "whatever," which gives the passage a sense of repetitive continuity. Third, within vv. 18–20, the promise about binding and loosing in v. 18 is connected to the promise about prayer in vv. 19 by the recurring phrases "on earth" and "in heaven."

It seems, then, that in 18:15–20 we have a passage that first instructs on how to reprove an offender, vv. 15–17, and then instructs how to follow up the reproof ritually by binding or loosing with prayer, vv. 18–20. To such an interpretation one might object that vv. 18–20 are formulated as promises, not as ritual instructions. Admittedly, before the sayings in vv. 18–20 were put in their literary context by the Matthean redactor, the promises may very well have been transmitted as disparate generally assuring sayings (cf. Luz 2001: 423, 448–449; Davies and Allison 1991: 752, 781), but when Matthew puts them in this context and binds them together with repeated catchwords, the sayings function as instructions. The greater part of the speech in chapter 18 (vv. 12–35) motivates and instructs on communal practices of reintegration and forgiveness. The verses preceding vv. 18–20 (vv. 15–17) contain instructions for reproof and the following verses (vv. 21–22) consist of instructions for forgiveness. That is, the literary context of vv. 18–20 is communal instructions. Assuming that Matthew for no reason whatsoever changes the subject in vv. 18–20 to general assurances that have nothing to do with the theme of the rest of the chapter does not make sense. It is more reasonable to assume that Matthew uses existing saying traditions to give instructions.

Within vv. 18–19, the repetition in v. 19 of phrases from v. 18 ("on earth," "in heaven") makes sure that the reader understands that the promise about prayer in v. 19 elaborates how the binding and loosing in v. 18 should be done – it should be done through prayer involving at least two or three persons. Thus, in its context, the promise about efficient prayer in v. 19 functions as a ritual instruction for how they should loose or bind the sinning brother. I will argue in this article that a loosing prayer functioned as a reintegrative ritual, and that a binding prayer functioned as a denigrating ritual.

The meaning of binding and loosing in v. 18 has been discussed unceasingly by scholars, but I suggest that that the cryptic words in v. 18 make most sense in the literary context of Matt 18 as a whole if "bind" means "not mediate divine forgiveness of sins" and "loose" means "mediate divine forgiveness of sins." Richard Hiers (1985) summarizes four types of possible cultural backgrounds for the terms "bind" and "loose" suggested by scholars – vows, authority to make halakhic decision, bans, and forgiveness of sins – and then adds his own suggestion that the language ultimately comes from the language of binding and loosing demons. What Hiers in my opinion shows is that the metaphorical potency of these verbs is enormous and that the range of possible associations to the terminology of binding and loosing is so wide that the meaning of the words for Matthew cannot be determined by inter-textual comparisons. Hiers himself speculates that Jesus might have used the words "bind" and "loose" in his exorcisms, but rightly concludes that if this is the case, then the meaning must have mutated before the expression was placed in Matt 16:19 and 18:18 respectively. Therefore, the expression must be understood in the light of the preceding and following verses. We should not even be too hasty to assume that the meaning of the phrase is identical in the two occurrences in Matthew. Even though binding and loosing can reasonably be interpreted as the authority to make general halakhic decisions in 16:19, the immediate context of 18:18 demands that the binding and loosing here somehow deals with specific cases of transgression, since both the preceding and the following verses instruct on how to deal with individual sinners.

Many commentators argue that binding and loosing in 18:18 is a judicial ruling of specific cases (e.g., Davies and Allison 1991: 787; Keener 1999: 454–455; France 2007: 695). Other commentators argue, in my opinion rightly so, that loosing is not just a judicial decision, but an act of mediating divine forgiveness (e.g., Luz 2001: 454; Gundry 1994: 369). The first mentioned commentators understand the verse purely as a judicial procedure within the community, that is, simply as a decision about right and wrong. "Loose" would then equal "declare not guilty." However, both the preceding and the following verses deal with the reintegration (vv. 12–17) and forgiveness (vv. 21–35) of people *who are guilty*. An interpretation of "loose" as declaration of innocence does therefore not fit the context. The interpretation that "loose" means liberation from sin, on the other hand, fits the context perfectly. The judicial interpretation, that loosing and binding means making judicial decisions, forces commentators to interpret vv. 19–20 either as general insurance that the decision in v. 18 will be valid and implicitly ignore that the following verse contains a promise about effective prayer (Davies and Allison 1991: 788), to understand v. 19 as an encouragement to pray for the future restoration of the sinner (Keener 1999: 455), or to assume that Matthew changes the subject entirely in vv. 19–20 (France 2007: 697). In contrast, if binding and loosing is not just a judicial ruling but something that has effect on the sinner, then the prayer ritual in vv. 19–20 makes sense in the context. The prayer ritual effectuates the loosing or binding of sin in heaven.

As I will argue below, Matthew 18:15–17 has a decidedly anti-judicial agenda in its interpretation of the Jewish reproof tradition. Moreover, as I will also argue below, sin is perceived, quite tangibly, as dangerous in Matthew's imagination. Therefore it fits Matthew's agenda and worldview that loosing means being liberated from the danger that sin constituted, and that binding means retaining the danger of sin. (Cf. the use of *lyō* in the LXX translation of Isa 40:2; Job 42:9; 2 Macc 12:45; Sir 28:2.)

Disintegrative and Reintegrative Shaming

A central part of the argument of this article is that shame is a key issue in the Matthean reproof practice. To prepare for that discussion, we must first elaborate on how shaming functions to reintegrate or disintegrate offenders in social interaction. Scholars generally accept that honour and shame were central to the perception of social life in the ancient Mediterranean world, and the research on the subject is extensive in New Testament scholarship (for bibliography, Pilch 2011; 2012). However, criminologist John Braithwaite's (1989) reintegrative shaming theory, where he distinguishes between "disintegrative shaming" and "reintegrative shaming," has never been used to analyse New Testament texts. Braithwaite distinguishes the two by the differing effects they produce on the shamed person:

> Reintegrative shaming means that expressions of community disapproval, which may range from mild rebuke to degradation ceremonies, are followed by gestures of reacceptance into the community of law-abiding citizens. These gestures of reacceptance will vary from a simple smile expressing forgiveness and love to quite formal ceremonies to decertify the offender as deviant. Disintegrative shaming (stigmatization), in contrast, divides the community by creating a class of outcasts. (Braithwaite 1989: 55, cf. 4.)

That is, shaming may produce either a) return to the norms of the community and reintegration, or b) marginalization and exclusion. Braithwaite, being a criminologist, is concerned with crime rates, and points out that crime rates are much higher in the United States than in Japan (61–68). According to Braithwaite's analysis, the legal system in the US tends to produce disintegrative shame, while the Japanese system tends to produce reintegrative shame. In the US, courts exact long jail sentences, while the Japanese offenders only rarely have to go to jail. Effectively, the US produces disintegrative shame and criminals are thus pushed outside the acceptance of society, which makes them likely to commit crime again. Japan, on the other hand, produces reintegrative shame through comparatively mild sentences combined with social pressure from peers. This is possible because the Japanese community is strongly collectivistic and interdependent. Much of the punishment for the crime is thus the interpersonal shame that being sentenced produces in relation to relatives, friends, and victims, rather than the formal punishment exacted in the courtroom. Importantly, the shaming is combined with an opportunity to repent and become reintegrated into the community of law-obedient citizens.

When Braithwaite wrote his book, evolutionary psychology was not as well developed as it is today, but recent research on the evolutionary function of shame gives support to his suggestion. Evolutionary psychologists suggest that shame increases fitness by inhibiting certain behaviours that would potentially disqualify us from the goods that having cooperation partners brings (Gilbert 2003; cf. Jaffe 2008). On average, shame guides social behaviour in directions that increase fitness. The capacity to anticipate what will cause shame is as important as the actual experience of shame, since our anticipation inhibits our behaviour before we have done something anti-social (Greenwald and Harder 1998). Shame can induce several different courses of action (Gilbert 2003; Greenwald and Harder 1998; Tangney and Dearing 2002). One domain of shame is shame related to behaviours counter to the norms of the group. When someone feels shame for breaking social norms, it often induces an impulse to repair relations by showing submissiveness. However, shame can also provoke an impulse to hide from the shaming gaze of the group. Shame can therefore both induce pro-social and withdrawing behaviour; in Braithwaite's terminology, reintegration and disintegration. Another domain of shame is related to competition for social status. When you have been shamed and denigrated in a contest for social honour, the most typical reactions are mortification, anger, desire for revenge, and longing to regain your honour. This kind of shame has been the focus of much New Testament scholarship (see discussion below).

In a later article, Braithwaite, together with Stephen Mugford (1994), elaborates on what elements procedures of shaming should have in order to be reintegrative rather than disintegrative. They enumerate no less than 14 factors, but here

I only summarize their argument selectively in a way that I deem to have heuristic value for our study of Matt 18:15–20:

> – *Shaming with an opening for reintegration.* The offender should be confronted with what s/he has done. However, the shaming should not be so harsh that the offender loses all hope for acceptance, and it should always be combined with the possibility of repentance and reconciliation.
> – *No identification of offender with offense.* The offender should be defined so that s/he is not identified with the offense, but so that the offense is something that the offender can distance him-/herself from. The offender is thus still seen as a morally capable agent.
> – *Presence of offender's kin or friends.* There should be people present who care about the offender and whom the offender care about. The presence of such people induces feelings of both shame and love.
> – *Mediator impartiality.* Third party process leaders should be able to empathize with both offender and victim.
> – *Inclusion ritual.* There should be a ritual of inclusion that reintegrates the offender.

According to Braithwaite (1989: 69–83), reintegrative shaming is much more potent than punishment to maintain moral behaviour within a community. Most people are more worried about what other people, especially people close to them, will say about them than about punishments. That is, the motivation to abstain from unacceptable behaviour comes more from shame than from fear. Punishment only reforms the offender if the offender sees the punishment as shaming. Harsh punishments also tend to become disintegrative rather than reintegrative shaming procedures.

New Testament research using the concepts of honour and shame as interpretative keys is massive (Pilch 2011; 2012 for bibliography), ever since the seminal work of Bruce Malina (1981; 3rd ed. 2001) where he introduced social-scientific models for these concepts, based on Mediterranean anthropology. Here I will limit my discussion to one remark: When shaming has been discussed in New Testament scholarship, shaming as a challenge that requires a riposte has been at the centre of scholarly discussion. Reintegrative shaming, however, has been a less explored topic.

Malina and many others (e.g., Moxnes 1996; Rohrbaugh 2010) have explored how shaming challenges, such as accusations, insults, or devious questions, was expected to lead to a riposte by the challenged person in order to defend honour. In the Gospels, for instance, Jesus wins all arguments with other Jewish leaders by successfully delivering a riposte to their negative challenges (e.g., Malina and Rohrbaugh 1998a; 1998b; Neyrey 1998; 2007). The by-standing crowd gives Jesus honour and his opponents have to go away in shame. In this game, honour is given to one at the expense of the other. It is "zero sum game," as Malina (2001: 89–90) would call it. With the terminology of Braithwaite, these negative challenges are very often cases of disintegrative shaming since the shaming procedure ends up in social distance and division.

Malina (2001: 33–35) makes a distinction between positive and negative challenges, where positive challenges, such as gifts and praise, is not intended to denigrate or hurt the other person, but just to introduce a positive exchange (cf. 2001: 95). Such challenges also need a riposte – a friendly riposte – in order to maintain honour. I mention this, just to clarify that Malina's model does not claim that all challenges are meant to rob an opponent of honour. However, neither positive nor negative challenges fit the concept of reintegrative shaming since neither form of challenge is described in Malina's model as a loving attempt to induce repentance or moral reform in the shamed person.

One example of a narrative scene that could be analysed in a new way with the concept of reintegrative shaming is Jesus' encounter with the Samaritan woman in John 4. Jerome Neyrey (2007: 93) uses the model of challenge and riposte to analyse the scene and rightly emphasize how Jesus and the woman challenge and riposte each other (cf. Neyrey 2009: 160–162). His analysis works well, all the way up until the point where he has to explain why the scene does not end up with Jesus "defeating" the woman, even though Jesus has insulted her life-style in a rather harsh manner. When the outcome of the dialogue surprises, Neyrey notes, rightly so, that "*Although* the Samaritan woman and Jesus play the game of challenge and riposte, he does not shame her and send her away in defeat. *On the contrary*, he rewards her..." (2009: 93, emphasis added). Jesus' challenges to the woman's lifestyle have inspired her to change. Here the concept of reintegrative shaming (in this case perhaps better called "integrative shaming") can improve the analysis. John has decided to describe the scene in a way that would be understood by his collectivistic readers to facilitate reintegration. Firstly, Jesus and the Samaritan woman are alone. That is, there is no crowd around them, so the verbal exchange does not aim to win the favour of an audience in the world of the narrative. This gives the woman opportunity to reform without worrying about defending her reputation. Second, Jesus does not claim that the Samaritan woman is a certain kind of person, but rather just states what she has done. "You have had five husbands, and the one you have now is not your husband" (John 4:18). Thus he gives her the opportunity to detach herself from her past actions, just like Braithwaite suggests one should. Third, Jesus combines the shaming with an integrating opportunity – to drink the water of life (4:14). Her response is overwhelming. Having been an outcast, she becomes an integrated agent for faith in the Messiah (4:29, 39).

David DeSilva is probably the New Testament scholar who has most frequently emphasized that shaming can be a device for intra-group rhetoric of identity formation and community maintenance (e.g., 1996; 2000a, 78–84; 2000b; 2009: 189–192). If certain behaviours are disgraceful and other honourable, shame will be an efficient motivator to make people conform to the standards of the group. DeSilva's analyses could be said to describe the dynamics of reintegrative shaming, although he does not use this terminology. However, his analysis can be further nuanced by several of the insights in Braithwaite's theory, for instance that reintegrative shaming a) should be formulated so that the shamed person can distance him-/herself from the shameful act, and b) should be combined with love, forgiveness, and openings for reintegration.

Louise Lawrence's (2002; 2003: 142–180) critical engagement with Malina's (2001) agonistic understanding of shaming is also of some relevance for our discussion. Zeba Crook (2007; cf. 2009: 597–599) has rightly pointed out that her criticism of Malina on this issue is partly based on a caricature of his model. Nevertheless, Lawrence is right when she argues that although the pattern of challenge and riposte is a valid interpretation of many disputes in the Gospel of Matthew, not all critical verbal interactions are meant as competitions for honour. Sometimes, criticism is just part of a negotiation or a dispute over common interest (2003: 168). Although she does not specifically discuss reintegrative shaming, the general implication of her insight is that criticism is not always a competition for honour but can also be instrumental in influencing the criticized person in a certain direction.

Matthew's Reproof in Its Cultural Context

The instruction to "reprove" (*elenchō*) a sinning brother in Matt 18:15–17 has predecessors in both Jewish and Greco-Roman culture. These texts have been carefully compared to Matthew's account by others (e.g., Carmody 1989; Duling 1998; 2011:212–244; Kampen 1998; Karkowski 2004; Kugel 1987), so there is no need for a complete survey here. I will only discuss a number of texts that demonstrate how the aim of reproof often, but not always, was to help a faulty person to improve.

Plutarch's advice about how one should admonish a friend, in his treaty *How to Tell a Flatterer from a Friend*, is a good starting point to understand reintegrative shaming in Antiquity. Plutarch uses vocabulary like "frank speech" (*parrhē-sia*), "admonish" (*noutheteō*), and "criticism" (*epitimēsis*) rather than "reprove" (*elengchō*) in his rather long discussion (*Adul. am.* 25–37). He thus adheres to the *topos* of "frank speech" (cf. Duling 1998; Fitzgerald 1996). As he argues that a good friend admonishes in private, not in public, he shows insight into the psyche of a person concerned about honour and shame (chs. 32–33). If a person is reproved in public, Plutarch reasons, his first concern will be to protect his honour and he will not be open for moral reform. In private, on the other hand, the reproved person can accept admonitions from a good friend, since he can trust that the friend's motif is to help him rather than to improve his own honour before the public at the expense of the reproved person. Plutarch describes a combination of shaming and care that is typical of Braithwaite's reintegrative shaming. The honour-game is called off, and instead the aim of shaming is the well-being of the shamed person.

Jewish texts about reproof usually allude to or quote portions of Lev 19:15–18, especially v. 17, "You shall not hate your neighbour in your heart. You shall reprove your neighbour and not bear sin because of him." These early Jewish interpretations of Lev 19:17 have been carefully analysed by James Kugel (1987). Kugel shows that several interpretations of reproof are non-judicial and informal, while other interpretations are judicial. The non-judicial interpretations motivate the reproof with care of the "neighbour" or "friend" (Sir 19:13–17; 20:2–3; *T. Gad* 6; *Sifra* on Lev 19:17). The scenario in these texts is private confrontation, probably in order to avoid public shame (cf. Prov 25:9–10). A partial exception is perhaps *Targum Ps.-Jonathan* on Lev 19:17, arguing that the one who reproves is not responsible for the embarrassment of the offender.

The texts which are structurally closest to Matt 18:15–17 are portions of the decidedly judicial Qumran penal code in D (CD IX, 2–8, 16–22) and S (1QS V, 24–VI, 1), which give instructions on how one should reprove offending community members properly (Carmody 1989; Kampen 1998). Just like Matthew, both D and S elaborate not only on the practice of reproof in Lev 19:17 but also on the "two or three witnesses" of Deut 19:15. Just like Matthew, both D and S argue that reproof before witnesses is a necessary step before bringing a case to the assembly (Matthew), the elders (D), or the Many (S). However, there is a difference in attitude in the reproof instructions between S and D, as John Kampen (1998) rightly notes. The instruction on how to reprove is more judicial in D than in S. In D, the concern is a correct legal procedure. (Some concern for the reputation of the accused glimpses in CD IX, 4, though.) In S, in contrast, the main concern of the reproof is the improvement of the offender. The members of the community should "reprove his neighbour in truth and humility and in loving kindness" (1QS V, 25). Consistent with care for the offender in S, the first step of reproof is private. The reason, although it is not stated in the text, is probably that a more discrete proce- dure will increase the likelihood of repentance, as reintegrative shaming theory suggests (cf. 1QS VIII, 16–20). D, on the other hand, with its more judicial focus, instructs that witnesses should be there to ensure that the reproof is properly done and does not seem to include a first step where the offender is reproved just by the offended (cf. Carmody 1989: 147–149). Thus S seems to reflect a more intimate community than D does, which fits the theory that the legislative portions of D originated outside of Qumran (Hempel 1998: 1–14). (In CD XX, 17, which proba- bly belongs to a later stratum added in Qumran, exhortations are said to be for the good of the offender.)

The Didache, which is related to Matthew, contains glimpses of a reproof prac- tice, which can perhaps be seen as a variant of Matt 18:15–17. In the instruction about the Eucharist, community members who are in a fight are excluded from the meal until they have reconciled (14:2). This is similar to the Qumran penal codes, where offenders are excluded from the communal meal for several offences, but only seldom excluded from all aspects of community life (Jokiranta 2007). However, as opposed to the Qumran penal codes, which often prescribe a certain time period of exclusion from meals, reconciliation is enough to be allowed to par- ticipate in the meal again in the Didache. Likewise, Matt 18:15–17 does not pre- scribe punishment of a repentant brother. Did. 15:3, which refers to "the Gospel," probably Matt 18:15–17, advises the community members to "reprove" each other and to stop talking to an offender "until he repents." As opposed to the vague for- mulation "he should be to you as a gentile and a tax collector" in Matt 18:17, the social sanction is quite specific in the Didache. Also, the emphasis in Matthew that every effort must made to reintegrate the sinner, is not visible in the Didache. The Didache could thus be considered to be somewhere in between Matt 18:15–17 and the Qumran penal codes in lenience.

Matthew 18:15–17 as Reintegrative Shaming

The extensive similarities between the Qumran penal codes and Matt 18:15–17 dis- cussed above makes it tempting to argue that Matt 18:15–18 is a judicial code of church discipline. I argue, however, that Matthew alludes to the genre of penal code and does a subversive re-reading. The goal of Matthew is to reintegrate the offender rather than to exact a proper penalty.

Dennis Duling (1998), in his analysis of Matt 18:15–17, argues that the Matthean community fits within the category of voluntary associations in antiquity, and as such is a "fictive kinship association." Voluntary associations occupy a social space somewhere in between kin and city; household and public space (Kloppenborg 1996; Harland 2009). "Where government and kinship fail, voluntary associations provide fictive polities and fictive families" (Walker-Ramisch 1996: 132). We should therefore expect the norms for interaction in voluntary association to vary between family-like and public assembly-like. (We have already discussed above how the Penal code in S reflects a more family-like community than D.) Matthew 18 persistently pushes the imagination in the direction of family relations, which compels the reader to understand the communal instructions in Matt 18:15–20 in a certain light. The terminology of Matthew 18 is not "neighbour" or "citizen," but household-imagery like "child" (vv. 2–4), "little one" (vv. 6, 10, 14), "brother" (vv. 15, 21, 35), and "slave" (vv. 23–34). God is depicted as a "father" (vv. 10, 14, 19, 35). The only exception to the family-imagery is that God is "king" in the concluding metaphor (vv. 23–34).

The imagination of being family probably influenced how a Matthean community member would understand conflict resolution. Cognitive research on forgiveness shows that people are much keener on forgiving kin than other people (Mullet and Girard 1999). According to evolutionary psychology (e.g., Teehan 2010) and game theoretical simulations of social interaction (e.g., Kim 2010; Hammond and Axelrod 2006), it is a most rational tendency for any cooperative species to forgive kin and friends more than other categories. Most probably, we humans are born with this tendency to be more generous and forgiving to kin and established cooperation partners, since this strategy will give a decisive advantage under most circumstances. This tendency was probably even more prominent in antiquity, where the norm was to be very forgiving within the family and resolve internal conflicts as smoothly as possible in order to maintain the collective honour of the family (DeSilva 1996: 171–173).

Given the structural similarities between the Qumran penal codes and Matthew, we may assume that Matthew was familiar with judicial interpretations of Lev 19:17. Perhaps such tendencies existed within the Matthean community. It is commonplace to suggest that Matthew has redacted previous traditions very carefully in this text (e.g., Luz 2001: 423, 448–449; Davies and Allison 1991: 752, 781). Matthew's strategy is thus to use familiar knowledge and reinterpret it. That was likely an effective way to transform practices within a community, since innovation is more easily accepted if it fits existing cognitive structures (cf. Roitto 2011: 112–113, 153–154).

Matthew has carefully placed the parable of the stray sheep (18:12–14) as the interpretative key to both the preceding and the following instructions (Thompson 1970: 245–251). As opposed to the parallel in Luke 15:4–7, where the sheep is "lost" and "repents," the sheep is a community member who has only "gone astray" in Matthew. The parable elaborates God's care for his "little ones" in the preceding verses (18:6–10) and elucidates the goal of the following procedural instructions – to "win back" (18:15) the brother. The point that the goal is to reform rather than to convict a sinning brother is then reinforced in 18:21–35, where the importance of relentless forgiveness within the community is hammered into the audience. We may therefore suspect that Matthew is here reinterpreting an existing reproof-tradition within the Matthean community, perhaps one similar to the one found in the Qumran penal codes.

Matthew chooses to use the word "reprove" (*elenchō*), which echoes the vocabulary of Lev 19:17, LXX. The parallel in Luke 17:3, in contrast, uses "rebuke" (*epitimaō*), perhaps echoing the philosophical tradition of frank speech (discussed above). When Matthew emphasizes that one should reprove a brother "when the two of you are alone" in order to "win him over" (18:15), the attitude is close to Plutarch's concern, discussed above, as well as those Jewish traditions that focus on the moral reform of the offender and therefore advice confrontation without mentioning witnesses (Sir 19:13–17; 20:2–3; *T. Gad* 6; *Sifra* on Lev 19:17).

The attitude in Matt 18:15 is quite different from the S and D penal codes, even if at least S shares Matthew's interest in the moral reform of the offender. As discussed above, the most important difference is that in Matt 18:15 the matter is settled "if he listens," while the Qumran penal codes insist that proper punishments should be exacted for offences (e.g., Jokiranta 2007; Hempel 1997 for overviews). Jutta Jokiranta (2007) has argued convincingly that the punishments were vital to the identity of the Qumran community. For most offenses, the punishment was not total exclusion, but exclusion from certain aspects of the community life and lowering of the rank of the offender (2007: 293). That is, imperfection was handled by lowering or raising the status of members according to their conduct (2007: 294–295). The social function of the punishments was thus to express which members best embodied the identity of the group and thus to express the identity of the group. We may suspect that similar thoughts flourished among members of the Matthean community, since Matt 18 is introduced with a question from the disciples: "Who then is greatest in the kingdom of heaven" (v. 1). Elsewhere Matthew warns that they should not use titles like "rabbi," "teacher," or "father," since they are all "brothers" (23:8–12; cf. 20:20–28). The lack of punishment in 18:15–17, together with the emphasis on forgiveness in 18:21–35, can thus be seen as a way to counter a Qumran-like hierarchical imagination of community in favour of a more family-like imagination.

Since the goal of Matthew is to "win over" (v. 15) the brother so that he does not "perish" (v. 14), it was probably a good idea to begin with a discrete encounter, in order to maximize the chances that the shame worked in a reintegrative way. As Plutarch (discussed above), correctly points out, public disgrace makes it much more difficult for a shamed person to reform. We get no information about how the reproof could have been conducted, but the focus of the reproof is the action of "sin against you" (v. 15), not what kind of person the sinner is. According to Braithwaite, it must be possible for the offender to distance himself from his transgressions in order to experience himself to be an acceptable community member again. We may thus infer that Matthew's practice of reproof focused on the sin rather than the sinner, since the end result of a successful reproof in private was that the brother had been "won over," that is, reintegrated.

In Matt 18:16–17, the language becomes more judicial, as the text mentions "witnesses" and bringing the matter before "the assembly." Dennis Duling (1998) gives a number of reasons for why this passage could be seen as reflecting a judicial procedure. First, all the similarities between Matthew and the clearly judicial procedure in the Qumran legal codes. Second, the casuistic formulations ("if .. then ...") throughout the passage, so typical of judicial language. Third, the language of "binding and loosing" in v. 18, which may be interpreted as a judicial decision. Yet Duling is hesitant, for good reason, to conclude that Matthew promotes a full-blown judicial practice. Rather, Duling cautiously suggest, Matthew aimed to

> check the assimilation of a tradition toward cultural norms and practices that are more judicial – traditions he shares with certain members of his authorial audience – by attention to the original motivation of the Torah tradition in the light of what he understands to be the meaning and message of Jesus (1998: 18).

As I have already hinted, I would like to take Duling's suggestion further and argue that Matthew counters judicial understandings of reproof within his community by giving judicial language an interpretation based on cultural ideals for how one should solve conflicts within the family. (As we have already noted above, Matthew is not alone among ancient Jewish texts to interpret reproof in a non-judicial direction.)

According to Matt 18:16, one should bring one or two more community-members if private reproof fails. Matthew motivates the practice with "that by the mouth of two or three witnesses every word may be confirmed," quoting Deut 19:15 LXX verbatim. In Deut 19:15 (and Deut 17:6) the purpose of demanding at least two witnesses is to avoid false accusations. In the Qumran penal codes, the interpretation of the function of these witnesses varies. In CD IX, 16–X, 3, the discussion is about whether witnesses to the same crime at different occasions can sum up to the required number of witnesses and what witnesses should be considered reliable witnesses to a crime. In CD IX, 2–4 and 1QS VI, 1, however, the function of the witnesses is to testify that the reproof demanded by Lev 19:17 has been properly done. The witnesses are witnesses to the reproof, not the crime. That is, the Qumran legal codes allow creative interpretations of the function of the witnesses. Therefore, we may suspect that also Matthew allows himself to be creative in his understanding of the "witnesses" in Deut 19:15 (cf. Davies and Allison 1991: 784–785). The function "one or two more" in v. 16 is explained in v. 17 – their function is simply to aid the first person in his task to reprove the offender and make him "listen to *them*" (cf. Luz 2001: 784). The plural "them" indicates that they are all supposed to aid in the reproof. The quote from Deut 19:15 can thus be considered part of Matthew's strategy to reinterpret a judicial practice into a practice that aims at the reintegration of sinning community members in a more family-like manner, by quoting and reinterpreting the very text used by proponents of a more judicial practice of reproof.

Bringing one or two more community members along increases the social pressure and thereby the intensity of the shaming. As Braithwaite points out, if the shaming is too strong, the risk increases that it will be disintegrative rather than reintegrative. However, as Braithwaite also argues, the presence of by-standing people who care about the offender and who the offender cares about can increase not only shame, but also the experience of being loved and cared about by the community. Thus, the presence of such people can result in shaming with even more intense reintegrative force. Since the text portrays the task of the additional community members as helping the offended to win the offender over, this is quite a plausible scenario. The fictive family-framework of the reproof probably enhanced the reintegrative effect too, because, as Braithwaite points out (1989: 69–70), when people are asked about what stops them from behaving deviantly, the shame before the family is statistically the number one motivator.

In the Qumran legal codes, the reproofs before witnesses are not really meant to avert the need for a public assembly. Rather, as we discussed above, proper punishments were vital to the identity of the Qumran community. For Matthew, in contrast, taking the offender to the assembly is the last resort if everything else fails (18:17). Only if the other attempts at reintegrating the sinner fail, one should take this final measure. This is quite understandable in the light of Braithwaite's theory. If Matthew's goal is reintegration, shaming before a large crowd runs the risk of being counterproductive, especially if the offender has not budged at previous attempts. The goal of the process is still to reintegrate the brother, but it is likely that a person faced with a large assembly of accusers might "refuse to listen" (18:17), that is, choose to distance himself from the shame rather than to repent. As Plutarch realized, "Unsparing rebuke before many people makes every infirmity and vice more impudent" (*Adul. am.*, 32). Thus, there is a risk that the reproof before the assembly works to disintegrate the offender from the community rather than to reintegrate him. It must be said, however, that we have no information about how reproof before the assembly might have been arranged, so if measures were taken to lessen the public disgrace, then we will never know.

If all attempts at reintegration fail, the offender "should be like a gentile and a tax collector to you [sg]." Commentators generally agree that this phrase is vague and that it is difficult to guess what this might have meant in terms of practical interaction. Ulrich Luz (2001: 450–451) gives an overview of scholarly positions: First, since it is only the offended person ("you" in the singular) who is addressed, not the whole community, it is possible to argue that it is indeed only meant as an concession to the offended individual, but it is also possible to argue that it is really meant as an imperative for the whole community and that the singular case is only meant to reinforce the responsibility of each individual. Second, what does it mean to be "like a gentile and a tax collector" so someone? The Gospel of Matthew contains both negative and inclusive attitudes towards these groups (cf. Karkowski 2004: 225–227). One possibility is that the phrase means public excommunication, but it is also possible that the expression means marginalization within the community without full excommunication.

I fully recognize how open for interpretation the phrase "like a gentile and tax collector to you" is, but wish to explore if there is an interpretation of it that is more compatible with the overarching goal of Matthew to reintegrate the sinning brother again. In the light of Braithwaite's theory, excommunication would distance the offender from the community and thus make the procedure more disintegrative. If Matthew is trying to counter a more judicial understanding of reproof, in which some community members have been too eager to exclude members in order to keep the community pure, then a vague formulation like this, rather than the more straightforward instructions to distance themselves from evildoers that we find in for instance Pauline texts (e.g., Rom 16:17; 1 Cor 5:9–11; Eph 5:7; 2 Thess 3:6, 14; Tit 3:6) and the Didache (15:3), may have been a way to soften the practice from exclusion to marginalization. The Qumran penal codes typically prescribe punishments that marginalize sinning members from certain aspects of community life without excluding them entirely (Jokiranta 2007: 293–295). We can therefore allow the possibility that what Matthew has in mind is to somehow consider unrepentant community members marginal until they repent. With this attitude, the unrepentant member would have continued to feel both shame and care from the community – unless, of course, the marginalized person decided to leave the community.

If we allow that "you" (singular) in Matt 18:17 is only directed at the offended person but not the whole community, then we possibly have an even more reintegrative situation. The offender is not rejected from the community as a whole, but only by the one he has offended. After all, a "family" only rarely rejects family members collectively, but rather tries to solve issues in the family as discretely as possible (DeSilva 1996: 171–173). The offender still knows his reputation within the community, however – he is the one who refused to listen even before the assembly – and thus continues to feel the pressure to change his ways in order to be fully accepted as an honourable person in the community again. I do not argue that the Matthean community never excluded community members. For instance, there was probably reason to exclude those who were a "stumbling block" to other community members (18:6–9). Nevertheless, Matthew's rhetorical goal in 18:15–17 is not to give rules for excommunication but to promote practices of reintegrative shaming.

Finally, it should be noted that in many ways the reintegrative procedure reported Matt 18:15–17 is quite an ordinary practice for reintegration of offenders. In the 1960s, before more formalized control systems became fashionable in the health care system of America, Eliot Friedson and Rhea Buford (1972) conducted a field study among physicians in a hospital. The relation between the physicians was egalitarian in the sense that formal hierarchical power-structures did not govern the interaction between the colleagues on a daily basis, not unlike the Matthean community. Friedson and Buford report how the physicians handled a fellow physician who did not do what he was supposed to:

> When physicians are asked what they would do about an offending colleague, the usual response is, "Nothing". Asked what they would do if the offense was repeated, however, they answer, "I'd talk to him". ... From examples we have collected, talking-to seems to involve various blends of instructions, friendly persuasion of error, shaming, and

threating with retaliation. ... If the offender does not mend his ways the offended man may enlist the aid of other talkers, either the administrator or one or two more colleagues. Eventually, if the misbehavior persists ... the offender may be talked-to by the Medical Director, or a formal committee of colleagues. ... [M]ost physicians are loath to vote for so drastic a step as expulsion on the basis of complaint of the few colleagues or the patient who have experienced them. Only the most gross and shocking deficiencies will do. (Friedson and Buford 1972: 193–194)

There is no reason to believe that the striking similarities between the clinic and Matt 18:15–17 exist because the physicians were devout readers of the first Gospel. Rather, the similarities are probably most readily understood as rather common processes of informal social control through reintegrative shaming in egalitarian communities.

Matt 18:18–20 as a Ritual of Reintegration or Denigration

Ritual theory has developed rapidly the last decades (Bell 1997; Kreinath, Snoek and Stausberg 2008 for overviews). An increasing number of biblical scholars have taken interest in these ritual theories in order understand biblical texts and history in new ways (DeMaris 2008: 1–10; Uro 2010: 221–226 for overviews). At this point, biblical scholars who wish to use ritual theory have to steer through a virtual smorgasbord of possible theories and carefully choose theoretical perspectives that have heuristic value for a particular problem. In our case, the problem is to understand how the prayer ritual in Matt 18:19 can function as a conclusion of the reintegration process in 18:15–17.

I have decided to use three types of ritual theories in order to understand how the ritual prayer in Matt 18:19 might have worked in the Matthean community: First, Jens Schjødt's taxonomy of different kinds of rituals. It is an analytical tool to categorize rituals by asking how the ritual is imagined to change the state of affairs. Second, ritual competence theory, which theorizes about the experienced efficacy of a ritual. This theory is cognitive and analyses the perception of participants in rituals. Third, Roy Rappaport's theory about ritual as a way to transmit different kinds of information. The theory discusses the social functions of rituals. Together, these three can help us understand the reintegrative function of the prayer. Other ritual theories would undoubtedly help us understand other aspects of how this prayer may have been functioned in the Matthean community, but these suffice for our purposes.

In the analysis below, I will assume that the Matthean community actually adopted the practices depicted in the passage. Unfortunately, we will never know to what extent Matthew managed to convince his community on this issue, but at least it is a reasonable assumption that the text influenced the community for which it was written.

A Crisis Ritual to Be Rescued from the Danger of Sin

Jens Schjødt (1986), inspired by Lauri Honko (1979), has proposed a straightforward taxonomy for rituals by asking whether the ritual transforms from and to "crisis level," "ordinary level," or a "higher level." The three most common types of rituals are initiation rituals (from ordinary to higher level), calendric rituals (from ordinary to ordinary level, sometimes protecting from crisis level), and crisis rituals (from crisis to ordinary level). In Schjødt's taxonomy, a prayer that looses the patient from sin would be one that takes the patient from a crisis level to an ordinary level, that is, a "crisis ritual." A binding prayer, however, retains the sinner at the crisis level. Schjødt does not suggest a label for this kind of ritual, even though it is in principle classifiable, but we may call it a "binding ritual."

Our simple analysis with the aid of Schjødt's taxonomy prompts the question of how sin is experienced as dangerous in Matthew – so dangerous that the very purpose of Jesus is described as salvation from sin (1:21; 26:28). In Matt 18, sin is portrayed as a danger so alarming that it is better cut off limbs than to sin with them (v. 6–10), since the alternative is "the Gehenna of fire" for the whole body (v. 9). Next, sin is likened to the dangerous condition of being a sheep astray in the desert, which suggests deadly danger (vv. 12–14). In the concluding parable of Jesus' speech, unforgiven sin is likened to a massive monetary debt that can potentially result in the most fearsome punishment, since it destroys the relation to the creditor, God (vv. 23–35). Elsewhere in the Gospel, sin is associated with bodily sickness (9:1–8) and demon possession (12:43–45). Moreover, sinful behaviour can ignite God's social reaction of wrath and punishment (e.g., 5:22; 22:5–7; 25:31–46) and exclude you from the Kingdom of Heaven (e.g., 5:19–20; 7:21–23).

The perceived danger of sin thus has two dimensions in Matthew: First, it is a social danger since sin may lead to a bad relation to God and other community members. Second, it is a bodily danger, since the body of the sinner may be invaded by sickness and demons and, ultimately, risks burning in hell. Gary Anderson (2009; cf. Roitto 2015) argues that the Jewish perception of sin was cognitively modelled in analogy with two cognitive domains in Antiquity: 1) it was like a substance that could pollute you and wear you down, and 2) it was like a debt that could lead to punishment. I suggest that these two imaginations correspond to Matthew's perception of how sin is dangerous. The imagination of a substance readily explains Matthew's perception of sin as something that can affect the body's health and make it vulnerable to demonic influence. When sin is imagined as a debt, sin is a social liability in relation to God and others (cf. Eubank 2013). This fits Matthew's imagination that sin affected your relation to God and other community members (cf. Runesson 2013).

This takes us back to Braithwaite's analysis of reintegrative rituals. As was discussed above, Braithwaite suggests that a good process of reintegrative shaming is finalized by a reintegrative ritual, which allows transgressors to distance themselves from the immoral things they have done. In Matthew, sin is certainly detachable from the sinning person since sin is imagined as a substance or a debt. What is loosened or bound in 18:18–19 is not someone, "whoever," but something, "whatever" in the neuter (*hosa ean*, v. 18; *hou ean*, v. 19), referring to actions rather than persons (cf. France 2007: 696–967). Thus, the tangible imagination of sin as substance or debt that can be loosed through God's intervention made the intercessory prayer a highly relevant reintegration ritual.

The Ritual Efficacy of Prayers by Agents Divinely Empowered to Bind and Loose

Robert McCauley and Thomas Lawson (Lawson and McCauley 1990; McCauley and Lawson 2002) have suggested in their ritual form hypothesis, which is a central component of their ritual competence theory, that our intuitive perception of the efficacy of religious rituals is based on our perception of how we perceive ordinary actions. Our minds cognitively structure actions in this way: a) an agent b) performs an action (with an instrument) to affect c) a patient. In religious ritual actions, we imagine that "culturally postulated superhuman agents" (CPS-agents) – in Matthew's case, God – taps into the ritual action and produces some supernatural effect. If the CPS-agent is most strongly associated with the agent performing the ritual, it is a "special agent ritual," but if the CPS-agent is most strongly associated with the patient or the instrument, it is called a "special patient ritual." Special agent rituals are intuitively perceived as more powerful than special patient rituals.

Some of the predictions of McCauley and Lawson's theory have not stood up to scrutiny (Ketola 2007), but their claim about what kinds of ritual actions are perceived as particularly effective has received substantial empirical support. Experiments confirm that the agent performing the action is important for our understanding of the efficacy of a ritual in two ways (Barrett and Lawson 2001; Sørensen, Lienard, and Feeny 2006): First, if the ritual is described so that the CPS-agent taps into the ritual through the agent (special agent ritual), it is perceived as more effective and permanent than if the CPS-agent is associated with the patient or the instrument (special patient ritual). Second, if the agent is considered to have special ritual competence (e.g., priest, healer, prophet, shaman), the ritual is considered more effective than if the agent is not.

McCauley and Lawson (2002: 13–15) do not consider prayers to be rituals. However, their analysis of prayer only takes some types of prayer into consideration – the kinds of prayer that do not performatively change any patient. McCauley and Lawson claim that after baptism all who are present know, just by seeing the public actions, that a change has taken place in relation to "the religious world" (their terminology for the divine realm) for that person. After public prayer, however, they argue, people do not perceive that such a change has taken place. That is, prayer does not fit into the schema of an agent performing an action on a patient. In some prayers, for instance prayers where God is praised, no patient is prayed for. McCauley and Lawson accept that prayers may be components in rituals, but they cannot be rituals by themselves.

However, what we see in Matt 18:18–20 is precisely what McCauley and Lawson claim prayer is not. The prayer there effects a change in the religious world; it binds or looses in heaven. We can only conclude that "prayer" is a broad term that covers a variety of religious speech-acts, and not all prayers can be analysed in the same way. Thus, although McCauley and Lawson's objection against prayer being a ritual is valid for certain kinds of prayers, I find it reasonable to analyse the prayer in Matt 18:19 as a ritual according to the understanding of ritual proposed by McCauley and Lawson themselves.

The ritual form hypothesis prompts us to ask the following analytical question: Is the divine efficacy of the prayer in Matt 18:19 connected to the agent (the praying person), the instrument (the words of prayer) or the patient (the sinner)? Elsewhere in the Gospel, the Matthean redactor changes the conclusion of Mark's story about the healed paralytic so that the authority to forgive sin is extended to "humans" (plural) (Mark 2:12; Matt 9:8). This can reasonably be considered an expression of the self-perception of the Matthean community as authorized to mediate the forgiveness of sins (cf. Davies and Allison 1991: 98). The promise in 18:18 gives authority to the binding and loosing agents – "whatever you bind ... whatever you loose ..." In terms of Lawson and McCauley's terminology, Matthew promises the community that the praying community members are agents with special competence to produce an effect in heaven. As discussed above, people intuitively feel that rituals performed by people with special God-endowed powers are more effective than other rituals. In Matt 18:18, God's agency is especially associated with the praying agent, which means that prayer was perceived as a special agent ritual. This gives us reason to believe that this kind of prayer was probably perceived as particularly effective in causing heavenly binding and loosing.

Rituals as a Way to Establish Social and Heavenly Facts

Roy Rappaport (1999) argues that one of the functions of ritual is to transmit information in communities. He makes a useful distinction between self-referential and canonical information (1999: 52–54). Canonical information is the cultural beliefs and values encoded in the ritual. Applied to the ritual of prayer in Matt 18:19, the prayer implicitly transmits a cluster of canonical information whenever it is performed, for instance that sin is dangerous but removable, that the community is in a positive relation to God and Christ, and that the community is authorized to bind and loose sin. Self-referential information is the information that the participants in a ritual send about their bodily and social status to each other when they participate in the ritual. As applied to Matt 18:19, participation in the intercessory prayer sends information about the commitment of the praying group members, that the person prayed for is in need of forgiveness, that the interceding person has qualities that makes him suitable for the task, and – most importantly – that the person prayed for no longer is unrepentant but accepts the order of the community. A binding prayer, on the other hand, makes the unrepentant status of the offender manifest in the community.

According to Rappaport, people who participate in rituals commit themselves publicly to the information transmitted in the ritual (1999: 119–125). In this way, the ritual establishes that people accept the moral obligations which the ritual implies. In the case of Matt 18:19, the ritual of prayer obliges the community to accept the sinning brother as a fully acceptable group member again. The stray sheep has been found and should no longer be considered deviant. The reproved group member, on the other hand, commits himself publicly to distance himself from his past misdeed. This takes us back to Braithwaite's reintegrative shaming. He suggests that effective reintegrative shaming should include some kind of ritual that signals the offender's reintegration into society. An intercessory prayer could definitely have that function.

How public did the intercessory prayer have to be in order to establish the binding or the loosing of a brother as a social fact? The prayer cannot be one person's doing but at least two persons have to "agree" on performing the prayer (vv. 19–20). Does "two or three" in v. 19 mean the whole assembly mentioned in v.17 (Luz 2001: 458), or just the two reproving brothers in v. 16 (Keener 1999: 455). The two interpretative options point to a dilemma whether information transparency or discretion in the process of reintegrative shaming should be prioritized.

Michael Suk-Young Chwe (2001) argues that public rituals often function to make sure that everybody knows, and that everybody knows that everybody knows. Certainty that everybody knows is sometimes important because people are often only willing to cooperate in complex tasks if they are confident that (almost) everybody else will participate too. In the case of Matt 18:15–20, a public prayer before the assembly would certainly maximize the distribution of information about the status of the sinning brother and the whole community would reliably know the social status of all involved parties. However, public intercession in the assembly would probably often be experienced as a major disgrace by the repentant offender. In the terminology of Braithwaite, a public ritual risks becoming a permanent stigma for the offender, which would work disintegratively.

As I have argued above, Matthew aims to soften reproof practices in his community, which might indicate that the Matthean community is under less pressure than it had been in its recent history when the Gospel was written. If so, a public intercessory prayer in the assembly might be unnecessarily costly for the offender (cf. Sosis 2004). When contemporary Swedish schools resolve problems with bullying, they sometimes gather the bully, the victim, and their parents, and give the bully a strong incitement to promise never to bully again. To demand that the bully declares his repentance publicly before the whole school would be unnecessarily cruel in most cases. Nevertheless, the rumour often spreads among parents and classmates that the meeting has taken place, so the information gets around anyway. Braithwaite (1983: 75–77) argues that this kind of gossip can be a more discrete form of shaming, since the offender knows that everybody knows, but without having to confront everyone. Therefore, I find it quite possible that the ritual of prayer in Matt 18:19 was performed in a small group of community members in order to moderate the pressure on the offender. There is an interesting use of "bind" in Sir 28:18–19, which illustrates how rumour can be as efficient as public ritual: "Many have fallen by the edge of the sword, but not as many as have fallen because of the tongue. Happy is the one who is protected from it, who has not been exposed to its anger, who has not borne its yoke, and has not been bound (*edethē*) with its fetters." The information of the offender's status would circulate among the members of the community even if the prayer was not a fully public ritual.

Conclusion

In Matt 18:15–20, the Matthean redactor combines and modifies sayings from the Jesus-tradition and plays on Jewish reproof-traditions in order to reinterpret how a sinning brother should be reproved and reintegrated through prayer. With the aid of Braithwaite's (1994) reintegrative shaming theory, we can see how the discrete confrontation and the possibility for offenders to distance themselves from their transgressions probably made Matthew's reproof procedure in vv. 15–17 more effective in reintegrating offenders than many other early Christian practices. A ritual analysis of vv. 18–20 shows that the Matthean self-understanding as empowered to loose and bind sins through prayer made the community experience the prayer in v. 19 as an effective ritual, either a crisis ritual that helped the sinner from his dangerous state of sinfulness, or as a binding ritual that retained the sinner in a state of crisis. At the same time, the ritual functioned to transmit both canonical information about the identity and the theology of the group, as well as self-referential information about the reintegrated status of the offending community member.

Enduring Shame as Costly Signalling

The Case of Public Confession of Sin According to Tertullian

Abstract

This chapter analyses public confession of sins according to Tertullian (160–225 CE) as an emotionally and socially costly signal of commitment to a religious group, early 3rd century Christianity in Carthage. Here "public" means "before the community of believers" rather than "before society in general." What group dynamic functions did the ritual have and why did people accept undergoing the shame of public confession of sins?

Tertullian belonged to the Christian community of Carthage and authored several texts at the beginning of the 3rd century (Barnes 1985; Dunn 2004; Decret 2009: chap. 3). Two of these were on penance, *On Repentance* (Lat. *De paenitentia*) and *On Modesty* (Lat. *De pudicitia*), reflecting a situation in Carthage in the beginning of the 3rd century where penance was an established practice among Christians. Penance (Lat. *exomologesis*) is for Tertullian a period of repentance (Lat. *paenitentia*) accompanied by ascetic deeds followed by public confession (Lat. *confessio*) of sins. Many community members seem to have hesitated to confess sins publicly due to the shame involved in doing so, in spite of promises of forgiveness, salvation and reintegration into the community. The present analysis contributes both to our understanding of the social history of early Christianity and to costly signalling of commitment.

How Does Shame Work?

Tertullian claims that many Christians avoid public confession since they "anticipate shame" (lat. *praesumo pudoris*) (*On Repentance* 10.1; translated quotes from Le Siant 1959). Psychologists describe shame as an emotion that makes you feel unworthy in the face of others, as opposed to the feeling guilt, which makes you feel negatively about certain acts you have committed (e.g., Tangney 2002; Tangney and Dearing 2002). Anthropologists, on the other hand, often talk about shame as the opposite of honour. Whereas honour is positive social capital, shame is negative social capital (e.g., Peristiany 1966; Gilmore 1987; Malina 1981). There is, of course, a connection between the emotional and social aspect since social shame often cause the emotional state of shame. Carlin Barton argues that ancient Roman discourse on shame distinguished between the sense of shame, that is, an inner sensitivity to what is shameful, and actual shame, that is, losing honour in the face of others. Displaying the emotion shame could sometimes lessen the social shame, since the display demonstrated a sense of shame (Barton 2001: 197–296).

From an evolutionary perspective, the emotion shame increases fitness by inhibiting certain behaviours that would potentially disqualify us from the goods that having cooperative partners brings (Gilbert 2003; cf. Jaffe 2008). As with all emotions, shame is sometimes a crude instrument that can misfire or become pathological. Evolutionary psychologists recognize this but argue that shame on average guides social behaviour in directions that increase fitness. The capacity to anticipate what will cause shame is as important as the actual experience of shame, since our anticipation inhibits our behaviour before we have done something anti-social (Greenwald and Harder 1998).

Shame can induce several different courses of action (Gilbert 2003; Greenwald and Harder 1998; Tangney and Dearing 2002). One domain of shame is shame related to behaviours counter to the norms of the group. When someone feels shame for breaking social norms, it often induces an impulse to repair relations by showing submissiveness. However, shame can also provoke an impulse to hide from the shaming gaze of the group. Shame can therefore both induce pro-social and withdrawing behaviour. Another domain of shame is related to competition for social status. When you have been shamed and denigrated in a contest for social honour, the most typical reactions are mortification, anger, desire for revenge, and longing to regain your honour. Such responses have a deep history: primatology, neuroscience and evolutionary psychology have all ascertained the evolutionary importance of such emotions to elicit behavioural responses and manage, maintain, strengthen, or subvert social hierarchies and power dynamics in human and non-human animals (e.g., Panksepp 1998; de Waal 2013; for a historiographical contribution see Burkert 1996; for a comparative and religious reading cf. Paden 2016).

Human societies often use processes of shaming to rear up their members and direct behaviour. Criminologist John Braithwaite (1989) helpfully distinguishes between stigmatizing and reintegrative shaming. When shaming is stigmatizing, the processes push the offender out of societal acceptance so that the offender distances himself from the group. When shaming is reintegrative, it is coupled with love and forgiveness. The offender is put to shame, but also welcomed back to the group and accepted anew. Reintegrative shaming as a strategy to reform offenders only works if the offender values his belonging to the shaming community. The period of shaming must be limited, and the intensity of the shame must not be too overwhelming. Forceful shaming strategies often result in stigmatization. It should be noted, though, that shaming can also function to manifest the values for the whole group, and may therefore strengthen the cohesion of the group, even if the offender does not readjust (cf. Marques et al 2001).

What is Cost According to Costly Signalling Theory?

Costly signalling theory encompasses several kinds of signalling, but I will here focus on religious rituals that signal intention to cooperate with the members of a community and to abide by its group norms (Irons, 1996, 2001; Sosis, 2003, 2004, 2006). For this purpose, a costly signal is an action which proves that a person is motivated enough to pay a price to be allowed to cooperate with a community. Such a signal must be hard to fake and costly enough to deter unmotivated and cheating partners, but not so costly that it deters valuable committed cooperation partners. An effective costly signal is typically experienced as more costly by uncommitted members than by those who are committed. In religious communities, costly rituals can fulfil that function. In the present paper, I will not delve into whether costly signalling is the evolutionary origin of religious rituals, which is a matter of debate (e.g., Slone 2008; Murray and More 2009; Sosis 2009; Pyysiäinen and Hauser 2009). Also, although I recognize that sexual selection theory, including mate-guarding, mate-retention, and infidelity avoidance behaviours, is important when addressing normative in-group organization (as even Tertullian himself acknowledges; see below), I have decided here to focus mostly on ritualized costly signals of in-group commitment, tied only indirectly to reproduction (for sexual selection theory in the study of religion cf. Slone and Van Slyke 2015).

For our discussion of public confession of sin as costly signalling, we need to grasp what "cost" means when a ritual is analysed by scholars as a costly signal of commitment. To my knowledge, no comprehensive historico-anthropological analysis of what might be considered a cost in costly signalling has been undertaken. From my reading of Tertullian, at least four types of costs – that is, costs experienced by the person who undergoes penance – are conceivable:

1. Material cost, for example loss of property or bodily harm.
2. Social cost, for example loss of relations or bad reputation.
3. Emotional cost, that is, enduring emotions that we wish to avoid, such as fear, shame, or boredom.
4. Unverifiable cost, that is, all believed costs that cannot be tested empirically by scholars but may be experienced as very real by subjects who weigh costs and benefits. In Tertullian's world view, that cost is losing one's prospect of eternal life.

The most frequent examples in papers on costly signalling concern material costs, such as sacrifices or bodily hardships (e.g., Irons 2001; Sosis 2004). This is partly relevant to Tertullian's version of public confession of sins since confession should be accompanied by ascetic displays (see analysis below). Yohsuke Ohtsubo and Esuka Watanabe (2009) show that apologies accompanied by material cost (e.g., a fee) are considered more sincere than just apologizing.

Willingness to pay social cost is a fairly common type of loyalty test in religious groups, for instance cutting of relations with those who do not belong to the group. Public confession of sins works a little bit differently, since it might cause social shame (social cost) *within* the group rather than in relation to people outside the groups. I have not been able to find a costly signalling analysis of this kind of dilemma, but it will become evident in our analysis of Tertullian why the signal works. We may note that honourable reputation highly important in antiquity, since honour governed all social networks, which in turn determined a person's material opportunities (Rohrbaugh 2010). Social shame can therefore be analysed as risk of material cost.

If public confession of sins induced emotional shame, which Tertullian's texts indicate (see analysis below), then there was an emotional cost to pay for the confessant. One example of emotional cost sometimes mentioned in costly signalling studies is the boredom of attending Sunday services (e.g., Bulbulia 2004; Hendrich 2009). From an evolutionary perspective, an experienced emotional stress that hinders one to do what is strategic for social benefit could be considered dysfunctional for the individual. It seems like many costly signals in rituals, such as painful, horrifying, and denigrating procedures, tests one's commitment precisely by testing whether a person is prepared to suffer these emotions (e.g., Fischer and Xygalatas 2014). In other words, costly rituals are often designed to go against our innate intuitions.

Tertullian promises eternal life to those who confess their sins and hell for those who do not (see analysis below). Such unverifiable cost may be very important in an in an individual's assessment of cost and benefit. Still, at first glance these believed costs seem to be of no relevance from an intra-worldly evolutionary perspective. Yet, empirical evidence suggests that belief in supernatural punishment increases group cohesion (e.g., Atkinson and Bourrat 2011; Johnson and Bering 2009; Johnson and Krüger 2004; Schloss and Murray 2011). Richard Sosis (2003) suggests that perceived unverifiable benefit may motivate the believer to perform a costly ritual, while the sceptic will deem the ritual too costly. The costly signal will therefore effectively separate committed from uncommitted members. Sosis also suggests that such rituals can reinforce the belief in these unverifiable benefits, so that the believer stays motivated. Sosis' analysis has been questioned by Michael Murray and Lyn Moore (2009), who argue that there will be a strong selective pressure for adaption to a more intra-worldly optimal assessment of costs and benefits, so that such signals would not be evolutionary stable. Nevertheless, history of religion is replete both with examples of different forms of confession of sins (see, e.g., Bianchi and Gothoni 2005) and people paying material and social costs in the hope of extra-worldly benefits. William Irons (2001) argues that we humans are creative in our interpretations of religious beliefs and tend to reinterpret religious convictions to avoid costs. Therefore, Irons argues, particularly costly rituals can only be enforced if two conditions apply: a) group leaders can punish those who refuse to undergo the ritual (e.g., by exclusion, marginalization, or fines), and b) the cost of leaving the group is higher than the cost of the punishment. In a later paper, Sosis (2006) emphasizes that internalization has to be combined with external sanctions for a costly signal to work. To Irons' analysis, we would have to add, with Sosis' suggestions in mind, that c) beliefs that unverifiable goods can be attained by sending costly signals can only be maintained if the leaders have the power to prevent alternative beliefs in the community that would allow avoiding the costly signal. In the case of public confession of sins, we would need a situation where the leadership can effectively preach its necessity and marginalize proponents of less costly interpretations of how God forgives.

Public Confession of Sins According to Tertullian

Tertullian had a radical bent which eventually led him to sympathize with the ethically rigorist prophetic movement called "the Montanists" in c. 207 CE. However, in spite of his increasing criticism of the bishops, he does not seem to have left the mainstream church formally (Rankin 1995: 27–38). Interestingly, *On Repentance* (c. 198–204 CE) is written before joining the Montanists, and *On Modesty* (c. 213 CE) after (Barnes 1985: 32–54). Accordingly, he expresses different attitudes towards penance in these two texts (Goldhahn-Müller 1989: 352–379; Posch-mann 1940: 261–369; Favazza 1988: 187–201).

Before we begin our analysis of Tertullian's account, we need to clarify that this investigation is by necessity an analysis of Tertullian's subjective assessment of the need for costly confession. As we will see, we may suspect that other members of Tertullian's church had different judgement calls as to how costly penance should be and who should be allowed to do penance. Tertullian is our only source to the debate, though, and the position of other parties can only be inferred through Tertullian's texts.

Game-theoretical Observations

Costly signals of commitment are part of cooperation strategies. Therefore, we start with a tentative and informal game-theoretical analysis of the rules of penance in Tertullian's treatises, beginning with *On Repentance*. In the first part of the treatise, Tertullian discusses the seriousness of a first repentance from a non-Christian way of life, followed by baptism (Ch. 1–6). One should not be baptized until one can lead a life worthy of a Christian. It is utterly disrespectful of the gift of forgiveness through baptism to sin again after baptism – ultimately a sign of "friendship with the Devil" (5.13). The first repentance is "the price at which the Lord has determined to award pardon." Before the actual baptism, the proselyte must go through a "first baptism," which is learning fear of God. "We are not washed in order that we may cease sinning, but because we have ceased" (6.17). The period of repentance (more than the baptism) thus functions as a costly signal sent by those who wish to enter the community of Christians.

From a game-theoretical perspective, we can describe Tertullian's rigid criteria for baptism – the entrance rite into the community – as the strategy to a) include a person into the sphere of trusted cooperation partners only after sending the costly signal of repentance and baptism, and b) to exclude this person as soon as s/he "sins," that is, defects from cooperation. This strategy would perhaps create very reliable cooperation cliques, but also cliques that would easily vanish, since most humans "sin" (defect) sooner or later. One of Robert Axelrod's (1997) insights in his game-theoretical simulations of cooperation is that if you simulate agents who occasionally make mistakes, non-forgiving strategies, such as "tit for tat," will be less efficient than strategies that forgive one or two defections, for instance "forgiving tit for tat" or "generous tit for tat," since non-forgiving strategies cut out good cooperation partners who make mistakes prematurely. ("Forgiving tit for tat" is the name of a strategy where an agent continues to cooperate with defectors one time before it stops cooperating, in order to avoid unnecessary cessations of cooperation caused by mistakes. "Generous tit for tat" forgives not only one but two times before it stops cooperating.)

Tertullian is apparently aware that his principal demand of post-baptism sinlessness is unrealistic, since he reluctantly admits in chapter 7 that there is a "second repentance" (lat. *paenitentia secunda*, 7.10) after all, and spends the rest of *On Repentance* explaining under what conditions one may be forgiven again after baptism. The second repentance is "for the second time, but never more" (7.10). This "two strikes and you are out"-rule is equivalent to "forgiving tit-for-tat."

As Tertullian admits one more chance of forgiveness, it certainly improves the community's probability of long-term cooperation, but is he generous enough? In order to estimate how efficient this rule might have been for maintaining a cooperative community, we would need to know how serious a transgression must be in order to count as a sin that one must repent. Unfortunately, Tertullian does not answer that. There are scattered references to different kinds of sins in chapter 7, such as fornication, eating food sacrificed to idols, and lack of love, but these references do not help us reconstruct what degree or kind of transgressions calls for a ritual second repentance. However, Tertullian probably did not have minor lapses in mind since that would have quickly excluded all members and thus evaporated the community. Here we must admit that lacking historical data prevents further from game-theoretical analysis.

We move on to Tertullian's treatise *On Modesty*, which he wrote when he had joined the Montanists. The occasion to write is that an unnamed bishop, probably the Bishop of Rome or Carthage, has set forth and edict, which according to Tertullian reads: "I remit, to such as have discharged the requirements of repentance (lat. *paenitentia*), the sins both of adultery and of fornication" (1.6; translated quotes from Le Siant 1959). Tertullian strongly opposes the idea that adultery and fornication by baptized Christians should be forgivable under any circumstances, and most of the text is spent proving that according to the scriptures these are heinous crimes on par with murder and apostasy. As opposed to his opinion in *On Repentance*, he specifically denies the possibility of a second repentance for such offences and criticized the mainstream church for practicing it (Ch. 20). He also introduces a new distinction between "sins unto death" and "sins not unto death," inspired by 1 John 5:16 (2.14–16; 19.10–28). The former is "irremissible" and the latter "remissible." Towards the end of the treatise, he becomes quite specific about what sins he has in mind:

> It is a fact that there are some sins that beset us every day and to which we are all tempted. For who will not, as it may chance, fall into unrighteous anger and continue this even beyond sundown, or even strike another or, out of easy habit, curse another, or swear rashly, or violate his pledged faith, or tell a lie through shame or the compulsion of circumstances? In the management of affairs, in the performance of duties, in commercial transaction, while eating, looking, listening – how often are we tempted! So much that if there were no pardon in such cases, no one would be saved. For these sins, then, pardon is granted through Christ who intercedes with the father. But there are also sins quite different from these, graver and deadly, which cannot be pardoned: murder, idolatry, injustice, apostasy, blasphemy; yes, and also adultery and fornication and any other violation of the temple of God. For these Christ will not intercede with the Father a second time, He who has been born of God will not commit them at all; if he should commit them, he will not be a child of God's. (19.23–26)

It is difficult to say exactly what unites Tertullian's unforgivable sins. Some are harmful for cooperation, others undermine the group's Christian identity, yet others are bad for the reputation of the community.

Tertullian makes a kind of game-theoretical analysis of why it can be destructive for the community to make it a general policy to allow repentance for adultery and fornication. With sarcasm, he explains that it is too easy to sin if you know beforehand that you will be forgiven, and that this will affect the whole church:

> The Pontifex Maximus, forsooth – I mean the "bishop of bishops" – issues this pronouncement: *I forgive sins of adultery and fornication to those who have performed penance*. Oh, Edict, upon which one cannot write: *Good deed*. And where shall this indulgence be posted? There, I fancy, on the very doors and under the very titles of debauchery. Penitence such as this should be promulgated where the sin itself will be committed. There one should read the pardon where one enters with its hope. But instead of this it is read in the Church and it is promulgated in Church – and the Church is a virgin! Far, far from the bride of Christ be such a proclamation! (1.6–8)

Tertullian identifies the most basic game-theoretical problem of forgiveness: Those who forgive without restriction will easily be exposed to free-riders (Axelrod 1997; McCullough 2008). His solution can be described in game-theoretical language like this: Stop cooperating unconditionally with those who commit acts that are particularly damaging to the community. Cooperate again with minor defectors if they are willing to pay the cost of repentance. This strategy would probably work better than the strategy suggested in *On Repentance*, although it is harsh for those who commit "sins unto death."

The burning issue of *On Modesty* is whether adultery and fornication should be considered irremissible. Tertullian is our only source to this conflict, but we can infer the position of Tertullian's opponent through the text. Apparently, the unnamed bishop makes a different judgment call than Tertullian does. Although coeval Roman legislation sanctioned monogamous marriage, sexual relationships with slaves, prostitutes, or concubines were not prohibited and, albeit criticized, such relationships were available to free males as "a pivotal mechanism for reconciling formal marital egalitarianism ('one man, one wife') with effective reproductive inequality that mirrored abiding resource inequality" (Scheidel 2011: 113; cf. Johnson and Ryan 2005). We may therefore suspect that it was quite common that gentile free male converts did not adapt to the stricter sexual morality of the church. Consequently, the edict of the bishop, where adulterers and fornicators could be reintegrated into the community after due repentance, may have been a more functional adaptation than Tertullian's to the strategic situation of the church. Maybe the bishop deemed that irrevocable condemnation would cut off valuable cooperation partners too hastily, and that repentance was enough to maintain the moral standards of the church. We may also suspect that Tertullian could not care less about what was strategic in this case.

Public Confession as Costly Signalling in Tertullian's Treatises

Our next step is to analyse the costs and benefits of penance, as described by Tertullian. Was it a functional costly signal that deterred the less committed but not the uncommitted so as to create a functional cooperative environment?

Tertullian's estimation of unverifiable costs and benefits of confessing sins is straightforward:

> If you shrink from *exomologesis* [i.e., repentance and public confession], then mediate in your heart on hell which exomologesis will extinguish for you. Picture to yourself, first of all, how great this punishment is so that you will not hesitate to use the means which you have to escape it. (*On Repentance* 12.1)

Tertullian frequently uses cost-language to describe the trade-off between the shame of confessing sins and God's favour, for instance: "And the price (lat. *pretium*) which the Lord has set on the purchase of pardon is this – He offers impunity to be bought in exchange for (lat. *conpensatione redimendam*) penitence" (*On Repentance* 6.4). Gösta Hallonsten (1982; 1984) has argued that this language should not be mistaken for legalism. Rather than legal satisfaction, Tertullian demands gestures of good will towards God. In commitment signalling terms, Hallonsten's theological analysis translates to Tertullian compelling Christians to send a costly signal of commitment.

From the perspective of the individual contemplating whether to repent or not, the math is easy. Repentance and forgiveness is the difference between eternal life and eternal death, Tertullian reminds the hesitant (e.g., *On Repentance* 12.1).

The reward for sending the costly signal is ∞ and the cost of refusing is ∞, no matter what the temporary material, social and emotional costs are. As noted above, beliefs in supernatural punishment increase group cohesion. The belief in infinite unverifiable reward or punishment was probably highly motivating for some Christians in Tertullian's time – but not motivating enough for all apparently, since Tertullian has to convince his readers.

Tertullian is well aware that the emotional and social shame of public confession is experienced as having such a high cost that some hesitate to confess in spite of its leading to eternal life. He amusingly compares it to going to the doctor having caught what seems to be a venereal disease:

> Most men, however, shun this duty as involving the public exposure of themselves, or they put it off from day to day, thinking more about their shame, it seems to me, than about their salvation. They are like men who have contracted some disease in the private parts of the body, who conceal this from the knowledge of the physicians and thus preserve their modesty but lose their lives. It is, I suppose, unbearable to shame that it should offer satisfaction to the Lord after He has been offended, and it should enter once more into the possession of that salvation which has been wasted. Oh you are a brave fellow, surely, in your shyness – wearing a bold front for sin, a bashful one for pardon! As for me, I have no room for shame when I profit at its expense and when shame itself exhorts a man, as it were, and says to him: 'Regard med not! For thy sake it is better that I be lost.' (*On Repentance* 10.1–3)

Tertullian's psychological insights into how the human capacity to anticipate shame effectively makes people avoid confession is realistic, given the research on shame referred above. (Irenaeus, *Against the Heresies*, 1.13.7, writing in c. 180 CE, gives us another example. He mentions women who would not confess their sin of associating with a certain "heretic" named Marcus publicly, since "they were ashamed," which led to their leaving the church). However, shame is precisely the cost he wants them to pay to show their good will: "...by penitence God is appeased. Exomologesis, then, is a discipline which leads a man to prostrate and humble himself (lat. *prosternendi et humilificandi hominis*). It ... appeals to pity." (*On Repentance* 9.2–3). In other words, commitment to faith is shown by enduring shame.

In addition to the shame involved in public confession, Tertullian demands a number of ascetic practices, which are both humiliating and physically costly:

> [Penance] prescribes a way of life which, even in the matter of food and clothing, appeals to pity. It bids him to lie in sackcloth and ashes, to cover his body with filthy rags, to exchange sin for suffering. Moreover, it demands that you know only such food and drink as is plain; this means it is taken for the sake of your soul, not your belly. It requires that you habitually nourish prayer by fasting, that you sigh and weep and groan day and

night to the Lord your God, that you prostrate yourself at the feet of the priests and kneel before the beloved of God, making all the brethren commissioned ambassadors of your prayer for pardon. (*On Repentance* 9.4)

Later on, he argues that people 'are afraid of the bodily mortification' (*On Repentance* 11.1) just described. In a burst of irony, he explains how unconvincing repentance is if it not accompanied by visible costly signals:

Well, is it fitting that we beg pardon for sins in scarlet and purple? Come, then, bring a pin to part the hair and powder to polish the teeth and scissors to trim the nails and, if any meretricious beauty, any artificial bloom may be had, hasten to apply it to the lips and cheeks! Yes, and seek out baths of greater luxury, sequestered in garden spots or by the sea. Multiply expenses, search for the rich, gross flesh of fatted fowls, refine old wine and, if anyone should ask you make a good cheer, then say to him: I "have sinned against the lord. I am in danger of perishing forever. Therefore am I now weakened and wasted and tormented, so that I may win for myself the pardon of God whom I have injured by my sin!" (*On Repentance* 11.2–3)

Our first impression of Tertullian's rhetoric, then, is that all benefits of repentance (eternal life) are unverifiable, but all costs are intra-worldly. As we discussed above, human creativity in avoiding cost should according to Irons (2001) lead to attempts to reinterpret the theological necessity of repentance and public confession, unless the leadership can enforce the cost by punishing those who refuse.

We know from other texts from the first three centuries that Christian culture was not uniform in its rituals of confession (Dallen 1986; Doskocil 1958; Goldhahn-Müller 1989). In the Didache (4:14; 14:1) confession of sins is a collective recital. Matthew (18:15–17) advises procedures where sinning community members are first confronted in private. 1 John (1:9) and James (5:16) admonish individuals to confess sins publicly, like Tertullian. Hermas (Vision 1; Similitude 2.1.5; 9.23.4) portrays private confessions. Sometimes confession is portrayed as repeated practice (e.g., Didache 4:14; 14:1; 1 John 1:9; 1 Clement 51–52; 2 Clement 8), sometimes as limited to one occasion, just like Tertullian's *On Repentance* (Hermas, Vision 2.2; Hermas, Mandate 4.3), sometimes as impossible for certain offenses, like Tertullian's *On Modesty* (Hebrews 6:4–6; 10:24–30). In short, no stable long-term equilibrium for the practice developed. Rather, the practice was constantly renegotiated depending on local circumstances (that are not always easy to reconstruct from available historical records).

Still, Tertullian's texts reflect a context where public confession was an established reintegrating ritual for a number of years, although the specific rules of the ritual were obviously under negotiation. Why was it possible to maintain practice of such a costly ritual at this particular time?

As we discussed above, Irons (2001) argues that for a costly ritual to be upheld, the leadership must be able to enforce the signal by inferring even higher costs on those who refuse. In the church described by Tertullian, the leadership had such power. Only the community, as represented by the priests and the bishop, can mediate forgiveness, so there is no way around public confession:

> [The confessant should] prostrate [oneself] at the feet of the priests and kneel before the beloved of God, making all the brethren commissioned ambassadors of your prayer for pardon. (*On Repentance* 9.4)

> Where there are two together, there is the Church – and the Church is Christ. When, therefore, you stretch forth your hands to the knees of the brethren, you are in touch with Christ and you win the favour of Christ by your supplications. ... Is it better to be condemned in secret than to be absolved in public? (*On Repentance* 10.6, 8)

I agree with Goldhahn-Müller (1989: 356–366), that although Tertullian does not explicitly mention excommunication of those who refuse to confess in *On Repentance*, it is inconceivable that Tertullian did not have this in mind, too, when he warns about divine consequences. In *On Modesty* Tertullian explicitly talks about excommunication of sinners (1.20). Although Tertullian denies the validity of a second repentance for irremissible sin in *On Modesty*, he refers to the opinion of the bishops: "The Church has the power of forgiving sins" (21.7; cf. Ch. 10–13). The bishop as representative of the church claims authority to mediate God's forgiveness (21.17; cf.18.18), and most probably also to excommunicate those who refused to undergo penance.

Tertullian also criticizes the folk belief that soon-to-be martyrs have special power to influence God's forgiveness through intercessory prayer (*On Modesty* 22.1–4). This innovative idea could be seen as an attempt to bypass the leadership's monopoly on forgiveness through martyrs. Unfortunately, he does not inform us whether the leadership approved of the practice, but probably they did not. In short, Tertullian gives the impression that the leadership of the community had the power to enforce public confession. The price for not confessing sin was excommunication. Thus, all the benefits of confession are not unverifiable after all, since integration into the community, which means access to its social network, is a substantial intra-worldly benefit.

Differing Experiences of Risk Depending on Commitment

Tertullian pleas for why public confession of sins should not be considered as dangerous as it seems by appealing to how socially close the confessor is to his community. The confessant does not have to be afraid of stigmatization, since the community will show empathy with the confessant, he argues:

> If ever the danger to shame is serious, this is certainly the case when it stands in the presence of insult and mockery, when one man is exalted through another's ruin, when one ascends over another who is laid low. But among brethren and fellow-servants, where there is one hope, fear, joy, sorrow, suffering, because there is one Spirit from one Lord and Father, why do you think these men are any[thing] different from yourself (lat. *hos aliud quam te opinaris*)? Why do you flee, as of scoffers, those who share your misfortunes? The body cannot rejoice at the suffering of a single of its members; the whole body must needs suffer along with it and help in its cure. (*On Repentance* 10; cf. *On Modesty* 3)

This is an excellent example of what Braithwaite (1989, introduced above) calls "reintegrative shaming." The confessant can feel the care from the community as he confesses and reintegrated into the community again. To those strongly committed, the shaming ritual of confession was probably experienced as limited suffering worth enduring to avoid exclusion, since he could trust that the community would feel empathy for his situation and not abuse his confession.

A less committed member, however, might have felt less confidence in the loving goodness of the "brothers" and reckoned the value of reintegration lower – the risks of his confession being used against him as costlier than the benefit of being allowed to remain in the community – even if s/he believed in Christ as his/her saviour.

As discussed above, shame can both give the impulse to reconcile through submissive displays and the impulse to withdraw, depending on how important the relation is. We can therefore conclude that public confession indeed functioned as a costly signal that stigmatized and deterred the less committed but reintegrated the committed. The cost-benefit-analysis would have led to radically different estimates depending on the degree of commitment. By exploiting the human action impulses associated with shame, penance effectively induced different choices, depending on commitment.

Is the degree of cost which Tertullian suggests was well balanced? One of the more important qualifications of costly signalling theory is that a signal should not be so high that it deters more cooperation partners than necessary (Sosis 2003). On the other hand, the costlier the signal, the higher the average commitment of the members, costly signalling theory predicts (Sosis 2004; 2006). In the social situation of Tertullian's church, it was probably effective to demand high commitment from its members since the church was under strong pressure from society (Dunn 2004: 39–45; cf. Iannaccone 1994). According to Tertullian, Christians could be tortured and killed for their faith (e.g., *Apology; To the Heathens; To the Martyrs*). Only highly committed members could give each other the emotional support needed not to conform to societal demands, such as attending religious festivals (e.g., *On Idolatry*). A high degree of commitment was not only a matter of enduring, but also of living a life that supported the evangelizing efforts of the church: "The oftener we are mown down by you, the more in number we grow; the blood of Christians is seed" (*Apology* 50).

We may therefore expect that public confession disappears as Christian communities are under less pressure. This is indeed the case, for the church gradually limited the practice of individual public confession, and in the 7th century private confession before a priest was established as the norm (Dallen 1986; McNeill and Gamer 1938: 3–75).

Does Public Confession of Sins Increase Commitment?

Costly signalling theory mainly analyses religious rituals as tests of commitment. Sosis (2004; 2006), however, suggests that the very same ritual which tests commitment can also *increase* commitment, which contributes to the stability of the group. Tertullian does not dwell on how penance may increase the commitment of the penitent, but notes than penance is "warning others by its exemplary shame" (*On Modesty* 3.5). It is well established that high investments into any project or lifestyle increases commitment (Shaw 1976). Moreover, as we noted at the beginning of this analysis, pointing out what deviance is among the members of the community functions to strengthen the identity of the whole group (Marques et al. 2001). Also, we may assume that a ritual practice which manifests the saving power of the community as Christ's body would make the narrative rationale (Bar-Tal 1990) of belonging to the community salient. Most importantly, a ritual of repentance expresses a will to abide by the standards of the community, which typically would increase commitment to the group.

Conclusion

This study, which analyses Tertullian's view on the ritual of public confession of sin in the light of costly signalling of commitment, contributes to our understanding of said ritual in early Christianity and gives new historiographical boost to such theoretical framework. Costly signalling theory in combination with psychological insights on shame highlights how the shaming element of the ritual described by Tertullian induced submissive reconciliatory impulses in committed members but withdrawing impulses in less committed members. Moreover, our analysis of costs and benefits of public confession of sins suggests that the ritual could only become a stable costly signal under conditions where a) it was rational for the community to only allow highly committed members in the community, and b) the leaders of the community had enough control over the group to be able to punish those who refused with exclusion.

Our analysis of Tertullian also gives interesting input to the scholarly debate about costly signalling. Since it is just a case study, it is not enough to claim any kind of generality, but the results of the study can give some support for certain interpretations of the theory. First, by showing the instability of the ritual in early Christianity, it highlights how costly signals are constantly renegotiated through history, depending on the needs and power structures of the community. Tertullian's texts and other early Christian texts give us the impression of constant renegotiation rather than stability. Also, our game-theoretical analysis of Tertullian's rules of who is allowed to repent (that is, send a costly signal and thus be reintegrated) underscores how difficult it is to formulate stable costly signals and cooperation strategies in real life communities.

Secondly, the study underscores the analytical value of understanding 'cost' as not just material cost, but as experienced cost, which can be more or less correlated with material costs. We saw that the central aspects of cost in confessing sins were emotional stress and social risk – shame. These experienced costs could be indicators of material costs, but not necessarily. If cost is experienced cost, it can better explain why a signal can be costly enough to deter uncommitted people even if the benefit of belonging to the community is higher than the direct material cost of the signal. However, the study also suggests that beliefs in unverifiable benefits (in this case, eternal life) is indeed motivating, but not always motivating enough to inspire people to send costly signals, since theological beliefs about how one can gain unverifiable goods can always be reinterpreted. Therefore, the intra-worldly benefits (in this case, belonging to the community) must at least partly compare to the cost of sending the signal for people to pay the cost. Had not the leadership been in a position to punish people who refused to confess with excommunication, transgressors would probably have adopted a theology of forgiveness that did not require public confession of sins, in order to avoid the cost. The innovation that one could be forgiven by martyrs, which Tertullian rebuts, exemplifies attempts to avoid the cost.

Acknowledgement: The research for this article was funded by the Swedish Research Council, grant nr. 2016-023.

The Johannine Information War

*A Social Network Analysis of the Information
Flow Between Johannine Assemblies as Witnessed
by 1–3 John*

Introduction

In spite of the visionary Johannine ideal of unity in Christ in the farewell speech
of the Gospel of John (chs. 14–17), we meet a community that is struggling with
unity in the Johannine letters. The present study uses social network analysis heu-
ristically (Esler 2005; Theissen 2007) to understand how the Johannine letters attempt to establish control over the theological information flow in the open-ended
network of Johannine assemblies, in order promote a certain understanding of Johannine identity and theology while fending off alternative interpretations.

What Is "the Johannine Community"?

Brief introductions and commentaries to the Gospel and Epistles of John frequently use the term "the Johannine Community" without clarifying that the
community to our best knowledge is a network of assemblies, not one single assembly. Such undefined use of "community" gives the unfortunate impression
that scholars think of the Johannine community as one group gathered in one
place, which they do not. Scholarly reconstructions of intra-Johannine schisms
around the turn of the century emphasize the geographically dispersed character
of the community (e.g., Culpepper 1979; Culpepper, Anderson 2014; Hakola 2015;
Martyn 1968; Wengst 1981). I find myself in complete agreement with Raimo
Hakola's excellent analysis of the Johannine community as a rather loose network
with opposing leaders and convictions (Hakola 2015). The schisms that we glimpse
in the Johannine epistles are possible precisely because the community is not gathered in one place under a unified leadership, but rather in many different house-

hold assemblies. The most clear-cut evidence of this situation comes from 2 and 3 John: 2 John is a letter from the Elder to the "Elect Lady" (most likely a metaphor for a Johannine assembly, v. 1). The main errand of the letter is to urge the recipients not to welcome itinerant teachers with heterodox teachings (vv. 7–11). 3 John, a letter from the Elder to Gaius, complains that Diotrephes is not willing to welcome representatives of the Elder into his assembly (vv. 9–10). Just mentioned errands are only intelligible if we assume a community consisting of a number of local assemblies.

Alan Culpepper famously suggested that the Johannine network of assemblies was held together by a "Johannine School" led by the Elder (Culpepper 1979). This Elder was not the equivalent of a bishop, but led the Johannine School, which was comparable to philosophical schools. The School was responsible for the production of the Gospel and Epistles of John. As such, it exercised a doctrinal and linguistic influence over the Johannine assemblies. The evidence for a Johannine School at the center of the Johannine community (that is, network of assemblies) is inferential and therefore is somewhat speculative (Lamb 2014: 12). Nonetheless, the Gospel and letters of John cannot have been produced in all the local assemblies, and whichever assembly hosted the author(s) of the Johannine texts, must have had significant influence over Johannine theological thinking and language. The combination of, on the one hand, a distinct Johannine language, but, on the other hand, subtle theological and linguistic differences between and within the Johannine texts, makes the assumption of a Johannine school rather than just one Johannine author, plausible (Painter 2002: 75–77; Hakola 2015: 67–91). For that reason, I will refer to one of the Johannine assemblies in the Johannine community as "the Johannine School" in this discussion. In the epistles, we witness a situation where local assemblies are not necessarily willing to accept the doctrinal authority of the School. Besides the evidence from 2 and 3 John mentioned above, we see evidence in 1 John of a splinter group (or a group of apostates [Streett 2011], but that distinction is not important for the argument of this article) with alternative Christology who "went out from us" (2:19). Below I will discuss the position of the Johannine School in the Johannine community network and argue that it is probably not as central as it would like to be.

We should also add one more observation to our discussion of the Johannine community: contact with non-Johannine forms of Christianity. The reference in the Gospel of John to "other sheep" (10:16) and the recognition of Peter as the leader of the Church (21:15–19) strongly suggests that by the time the Gospel had been completed, Johannine Christians recognized other forms of Christianity as legitimate. We do not know the geographic location of the Johannine assemblies, but I accept the reasonable hypothesis that they were situated in the vicinity of Ephesus (Tellbe 2009), which is supported by second century traditions that place John's Gospel in Ephesus (e.g., Irenaeus, *Adv. Haer.* 2.22.5; 3.1.1; 3.3.4; Eusebius, *Hist. eccl.* 3.339.4–6 [citing Papias]). Ephesus as a possible location of the Johannine community allows for a certain amount of historical imagination (Cf. Tilborg 1996). If we accept the Johannine community was located in and around Ephesus, we may safely assume that they had other forms of Christian assemblies as their neighbours in the cosmopolitan city (Tellbe 2009; Trebilco 2004). We have solid evidence for the presence of Pauline Christianity in the city (Acts 18:19–20:38; 1 Cor 15:32; 16:8–9; 2 Cor 1:8–11; Eph; 1–2 Tim) and the author of the Book of Revelation found reason to address Christians in Ephesus and refute an otherwise unknown branch of Christianity called "the Nicolaitans" (Rev 2:1–7). Although we know very little about the movement of individual members between assemblies, it seems highly likely to me that Johannine Christians had exchange with other kinds of Christians in the area. Paul Trebilco argues that one can see possible signs of linguistic influence between Johannine texts and the Deutero-Pauline Pastorals (Trebilco 2004: 596–612). These interactions with other forms of Christianity further strengthen the conclusion that Johannine Christianity must have been a rather open-ended network (Hakola 2015: chs. 5–6; Lamb 2014: 200–205).

If our analysis points toward a loose heterogeneous network of assemblies in contact with other forms of Christianity, this means that we cannot mirror-read the dualistic opposition between "us" and "them" in the Johannine literature as depictions of an isolationist sect. Rather, when 1 John imagines a unified "us" against "the world," "the Antichrists" and "the false prophets" (e.g., 1 John 4:1–6) it is performative speech, meant to create a distinctive social imagination in a situation of ambiguous social relations (Neufeld 1994; Lieu 2008). Such identity-shaping rhetoric to structure one's social world is not unique to the Johannine literature but can be seen in almost any religious or political organization (Edwards, Potter 1992). The formulation of social identity does not have the force of description but of prescription, which in turn allows for identity-based decision-making and action (Roitto 2013; Hakola 2015: 118–146).

Johannine Leadership in Comparison to Other Voluntary Associations

The lack of formalized leadership structures in the Johannine literature is well recognized (Tellbe 2009: 183–207). Peter is acknowledged as the leader of the Church in John 21, but nothing similar to the institutionalized local leadership in the Pastoral letters can be found in the Johannine corpus. On the contrary, Johannine theology refutes the need for teachers since all members are anointed by the Spirit (1 John 2:27).

We do however get a few hints that point to individual leadership figures in the Johannine epistles. The Elder clearly enjoys an elevated status, since he can send letters by that title. He is not just an elder, but *the* Elder. However, it is also obvious that his power over other assemblies is limited, since he cannot command Diotrephes to accept his delegates (3 John 10). The anonymous sender(s) of 1 John implicitly attribute doctrinal authority to themselves since they have "seen and heard" (1:3), but nowhere in the letter do we find affirmation that the senders have any form of executive power over the recipients, for instance to exclude members. In all three epistles, the senders' influence seems merely advisory.

Diotrephes is our only example of a local leader of an assembly with some executive power to accept or deny itinerant teachers to his community (3 John 9–10). Diotrephes φιλοπρωτεύων αὐτῶν, literally "loves to be first among them" (3 John 9), according to the Elder. The meaning of this phrase is somewhat obscure and could very well just be an invective for Diotrephes' love for status and power. Yet I would like to suggest that the verb's πρωτ-stem echoes quite common πρό-terms (πρότερος and πρῶτος are formed from πρό, LSJ, s.v. πρότερος and πρῶτος) for leadership in inscription from voluntary associations. Titles such as πρόεδρος, προστάτης, and πρύτανις for the president of an association are commonplace (e.g., Harland n.d: inscriptions 7, 202, 269, 279, 288, 297[1]). If so, the aspirations of Diotrephes are quite conventional in the setting of voluntary associations. Perhaps the Elder envisions assemblies without formal leadership structures (cf. discussion above), but it would not be surprising if other local assemblies in the Johannine community chose presidents anyway, and Diotrephes seems to be an accepted authority in his assembly, given his power to reject visiting teachers.

Richard Ascough and Philip Harland have convincingly argued that first century Christian assemblies and Jewish synagogues were similar to other

---

[1] Note: To find a numbered inscription in Harland's database, search for "[number]" on the page, e.g., "[202]."

voluntary associations in the Roman Empire in their organizational forms (Ascough 2015a; 2015b; Harland 2009). Voluntary associations, including synagogues and Christian assemblies, typically had local leaders, but to the extent that there was trans-associational leadership, it was informal (Ascough 1996; Ascough 2015b). Associations, synagogues and Christian assemblies alike had varying degrees of exchange in the form of visitors and letters, but there is no evidence of trans-associational leadership with executive power.[2] This general impression of informal trans-associational leadership fits the Johannine situation, too. In his discussion of Ephesus, Ascough concludes that "there was no citywide Christian organization, at least until the time of Ignatius" (Ascough 2015b, 222). Whatever leadership there was between assemblies in the Johannine community, it seems that no one had the authority do force decisions on other assemblies. The only form of influence that they had was persuasive communication and informal relations.

A Social Network Model of the Johannine Communities

To understand what is happening in the trans-local communication between Johannine assemblies, we can use network theory. Said theory is at its core a mathematical theory about the relations between nodes connected by ties (i.e., dots connected by lines). While network theory can be used to model all kinds of relations, one of its most popular applications is social networks, called social network theory or social network analysis. In social network analysis, actors (individuals or groups) are represented by nodes and relations are represented by ties. In the network, there is a flow of content, e.g., goods or information, between actors (nodes) via relations (ties). A simple social network with six actors can for instance look like this (figure 1):

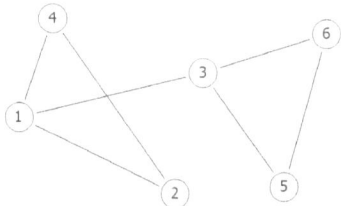

Fig. 1. Sample network

---

[2] The translocal Christian monepiscopacy gradually evolved from second to fourth century, see e.g., Sullivan 2001.

In the following, I will only present aspects of network analysis that are relevant to our understanding of the information flow between Johannine assemblies. Readers interested in a more thorough introduction are encouraged to read Charles Kadushin's introduction, to which I refer in the discussion below (Kadushin 2012). István Czachesz introduces the many different ways New Testament scholars can benefit from network theory (Czachesz 2017: 187–205). Dennis Duling gives a convenient overview of previous applications of social network analysis in early Christian studies (Duling 2013: 135–136).

Central to social network analysis are concepts that describe what nodes can influence and send information to other nodes most effectively. *Centrality* is one way to measure this (Kadushin 2012: 31–32). The node that has the shortest average distance to other nodes in the network is the most central node, which is strategic for a node that wishes to influence (i.e., disseminate information to) others. If the Johannine community had a Johannine School that continuously sent teachers to the household assemblies, then the School aspired to be a central node in the network. The scenario in which the Johannine School would have had the strongest centrality – and thereby influence – would be if all Johannine assemblies were solely in contact with the School but never directly with each other. All theological influence would then have come from the School (figure 2):

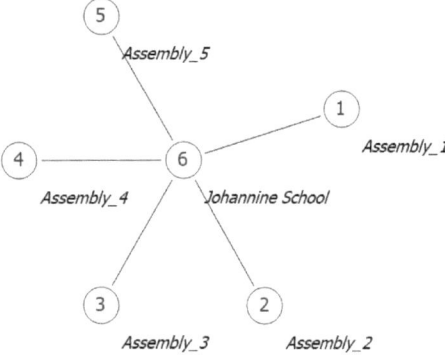

Fig. 2. Social network with the Johannine School in central position

A different scenario would be if the Johannine School was just one of many Johannine assemblies, who all exchanged theological ideas with each other through letters and itinerant teachers. This network would have higher *density* than the first network (Kadushin 2012: 29), that is, more ties between the nodes, and information would therefore be able to *diffuse* through multiple paths (Kadushin 2012: 135–161). The Johannine School would be no more central than for instance Diotrephes' assembly (3 John 9–10) and unable to monopolize the information flow (figure 3):

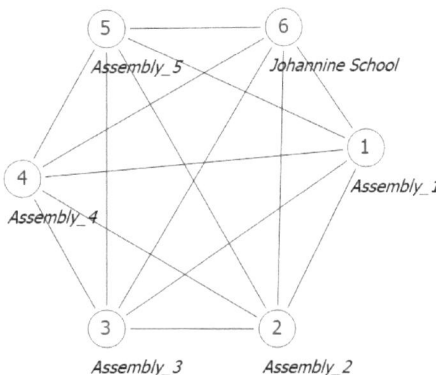

Fig. 3. Social network with the Johannine School in non-privileged position

These two networks highlight the tension between the beginning of 1 John (1:1–6), where the senders claim unique knowledge that the recipients need to receive and the theological assertion in 2:27 that all are equal in spiritual knowledge. The senders of 1 John make claims to the right to be the most central information node and yet they do not.

Since 1 John is a written sermon rather than a proper letter, I will here assume that it was meant for circulation to multiple assemblies. The recipient assemblies of 1 John are apparently still in contact with "antichrists" and "false prophets" (2:18–26; 4:1–6), since the letter makes such an emphatic effort to warn them. A reasonable reconstruction of the situation is that this schismatic group (or groups?) no longer is in direct contact with the sender of 1 John, but instead sends its own itinerant teachers ("false prophets," according to 1 John 4:1–6) to the Johannine assemblies. Let us call this group the Schismatic School, borrowing terminological inspiration from Raymond Brown's terminology "schismatics" for this splinter group (Brown 1979). (I only use Brown's terminology, not the specifics of his reconstruction of their identity. The precise convictions of the schismatics elude us, see discussion below.) Some congregations, for instance that of Diotrephes (3 John 9–10), might even be more interested in visitors and letters from the competing Schismatic School. If so, the social network of the Johannine community could for example look something like this (figure 4):

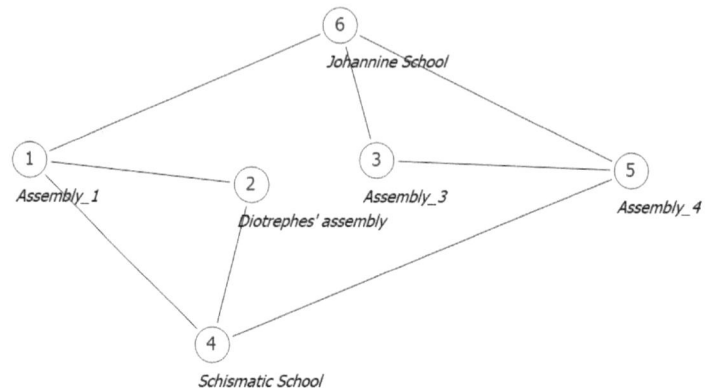

Fig. 4. Assemblies connected to the Johannine School and the Schismatic School

In this image, the Johannine School has no direct contact with the Schismatic School, even though they belong to the same social network. The schools compete for influence over Johannine assemblies and the Johannine School stands at risk of becoming more and more peripheral in the social network. Some local assemblies listen to both schools, some to just one. Some local assemblies exchange ideas, but others do not.

Before we continue, I would like to clarify that this reconstruction (as well as the reconstruction in the next section) is solely for the sake of a principal discussion about how we can understand the occasion for the rhetoric in the Johannine letters. We do by no means have enough information to confidently reconstruct the exact nature of the Johannine social network. The number of assemblies and their exchange of information is largely unknown to us, and all we can do is infer a possible situation from the limited evidence we have. Neither can we be certain that there was only one united group of "schismatics" that taught in one voice. Stephen Smalley, for example, identifies multiple groups of deviants in the Johannine community (Smalley 1984: xxiv–xxv). I am convinced that the interested rhetoric of the letters skews the picture of competing groups so radically that reconstructions of multiple groups and their teachings are impossible (cf. Lieu 2008) but given my argument throughout this chapter for the loose character of the Johannine network, the existence of multiple competing Johannine-like schools and teachers with their own version of Johannine-like theology is definitely possible. Neither can we know whether the three letters are occasioned by the same or entirely different conflicts (Lieu 2014). In principle, the schismatic "they" in 1 John could be a fictive rhetorical figure that clarifies the nature of Johannine identity by imagined contrast. However, it seems plausible that the very practical exhortations about itinerant teachers in 2 and 3 John do indeed reflect a real conflict. Aware of all these complications, I model one conflict with one competing school for the sake of simplicity and leave to others to reconstruct more complex possible Johannine scenarios. My principal network discussion and my principal argument that the Johannine school struggles to be central in its social network should be valid for many other versions of historical reconstructions, too.

Information War Across Weak Ties Between Local Assemblies

Mark Granovetter argues in a by now classic article that new information spreads across population via so called "weak ties" (Granovetter 1982; summarized in Kadushin 2012: 30–31). Granovetter distinguishes between *cliques* of *strong ties* between nodes that are densely interconnected and exchange information frequently and *weak ties* with less frequent information flow that connect these cliques (figure 5).

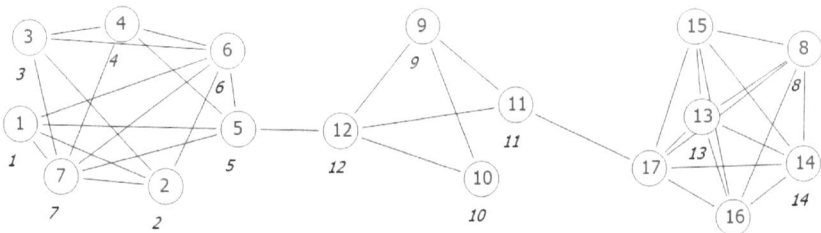

Fig. 5. Example of three cliques with strong ties connected by weak ties

The key point of Granovetter's argument is that cliques with strong ties already share most of their information with each other and will not contribute with very much new information to the clique, whereas weak ties allow for novel information from other cliques to reach the clique. Granovetter used these insights to discuss the importance of a wide social network to find job opportunities outside of one's closest sphere of peers.

Granovetter's insights have been used fruitfully by István Czachesz and Dennis Duling in New Testament studies to discuss the diffusion of Christianity across the various social networks of the Roman Empire (Czachesz 2011; Duling 2013). Czachesz argues convincingly that itinerant preachers, women, and charity created many weak ties that allowed for the gospel to diffuse to new groups (cliques) in new places. Duling, in response to Czachesz, agrees on the importance of weak ties but also adds that one must not forget the importance of the strong ties within for instance households for the recruitment of new members and stabilization of Christian assemblies.

In our case, the Johannine communities, we can use Granovetter's distinction between weak and strong ties in a similar way but ask different questions. The local Johannine assemblies were cliques of nodes (members) with strong ties. Within the assembly, the participants met rather frequently for worship. We can therefore reasonably assume that they shared knowledge about their local version of Johannine Christianity and most probably achieved a certain amount of local consensus. However, there was a certain amount of information flowing between the Johannine assemblies in the form of letters, itinerants and perhaps also copies of the (some version of) Gospel of John. Perhaps also other texts from competing Johannine groups and even texts and teachers from other branches of early Christianity circulated, but that goes beyond the evidence we have.[3] All these communications between local assemblies happened across social connections that in Granovetter's terminology qualify as weak ties. Novel information about other theological perspectives from other cliques is not as frequent as repetition of established beliefs within the clique. Yet, it is mainly through weak ties that new theological ideas can be diffused between assemblies. In previous figures, each node has been an assembly, but to appreciate the difference between weak and strong ties, we have to create a new model of the Johannine community where each node is an individual. The figure below (figure 6) is an example of what the community could look like given the analysis of the letters that will follow. (I imagine that there were more than five assemblies in the Johannine community and more than five to seven members in each assembly, but I do not want to make the network illustration unnecessarily complicated.)

---

[3] As mentioned above, Trebilco (2004: 596–612) has argued that there are signs of linguistic influence between Johannine and Pauline assemblies, but the evidence is far from conclusive, which Trebilco readily acknowledges.

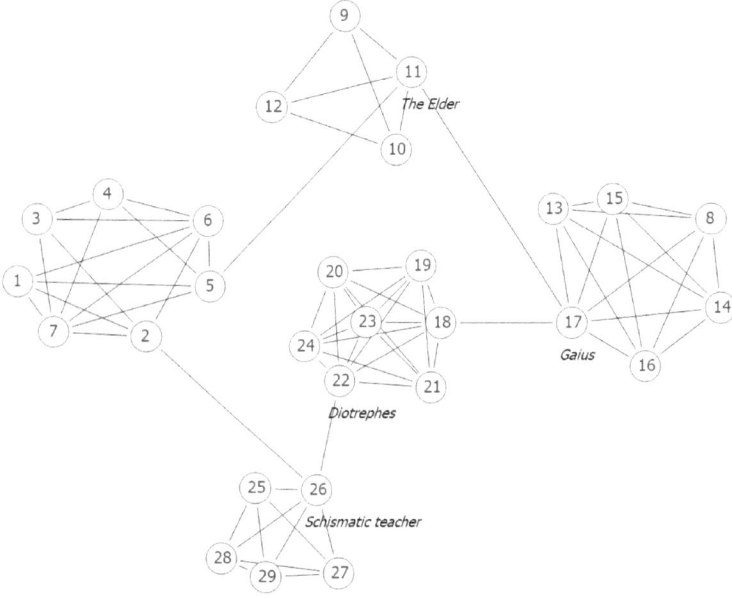

Fig. 6. Image of Johannine cliques connected by weak ties

The Johannine letters are communications across weak ties aiming to influence the recipient cliques in hope that the sender's understanding of Johannine theology and identity will gain foothold in the assemblies. But that is not all: The letters also aim to encourage the assemblies to cut off all weak ties with other groups so that the Johannine School becomes their main source of information. It is a battle for the weak ties. By cutting off ties between cliques, one creates *structural holes* in the network (Kadushin 2012: 29–30). Cliques that are connected to other cliques that in turn have few other connections can exercise greater influence over those cliques than if the cliques would have had many weak ties to other cliques (Kadushin 2012: 60–61). In the following, we look at each letter and ask how each letter both attempts to influence through weak ties and stop alternative influences from others by encouraging assemblies to cut off weak ties. (The order of analysis below does not reflect any attempt at reconstructing a temporal order between the letters. I just find it pedagogical to analyse the letters in in that order.)

2 John. The main errand of the letter is to urge the recipients not to welcome teachers with alternative teachings. It might be meant for circulation among several assemblies, since the recipient community is just called "the Elect Lady" (v. 1). The rhetorical strategy of the letter is straightforward: First, the Elder reminds the recipients of their shared social identity with the Elder and commends them for their way of life (vv. 1–6). Then he warns them that they can lose all this if they listen to the "Antichrist" (vv. 7–8). Finally, he admonishes them not to welcome anyone with false teachings (vv. 9–10) lest they participate in their evil (v. 11). If the rhetorical strategy of the letter was successful (which it might or might not have been), the Elder would have strengthened the weak tie between himself and the recipient assembly and at the same time cut off the recipient assembly's weak tie to the alternative teachers, thereby making sure that future influence came from the Elder (and his School) rather than from other sources.

3 John. The Elder's letter to Gaius contains no request, only complaints and gossip about Diotrephes. Rather than asking Gaius to do anything, the Elder informs him about how he sees the Diotrephes' actions. From the letter we understand that Diotrephes, similarly to the Elder in 2 John, attempts to cut off weak information ties from itinerant preachers by not welcoming them, preventing others to welcome them, and slandering their reputation (vv. 10–11). This time, the Elder is being cut off rather than the one cutting others off. In this situation, the Elder slanders Diotrephes back by calling his leadership ambitions "love of putting himself first" (φιλοπρωτεύων αὐτῶν, v. 9) and by calling his refusal to receive the Elder's delegates evil (vv. 10–11). We do not know Gaius' relation to the Johannine community, but apparently the Elder sees Gaius as an information backdoor (an indirect tie) into Diotrephes' assembly from which he has been cut off. It seems unlikely that Gaius belongs to the same assembly as Diotrephes, since he is praised for his hospitality toward the Elder's itinerants (vv. 5–8). Perhaps Gaius has a prominent position in an assembly that communicates with Diotrephes' assembly (as shown in the figure above). Perhaps the Elder writes to Gaius to insulate Gaius and his assembly from influence from Diotrephes by defaming Diotrephes' ethos. In short, the letter is a glimpse into an ongoing struggle between opposing members of the Johannine social network to keep one's own weak ties to local assemblies and to undermine the weak ties of competing voices.

1 John. The sermon in 1 John is much more than a response to the schism mentioned in 2:19, "they went out from us," and one should be wary of reading all contrastive language in the sermon as mirrors of schismatic opponents (Lieu 1991: 15–16). Rather, the sermon aims to formulate the identity of the Johannine community and demarcations from alternative teachings and groups is only part of that effort. Nevertheless, 1 John does contain passages that target alternative teachings and criticizes the proponents of those teachings heavily. As discussed above, we cannot know who these opponents are or to what extent the allegations against these opponents are fair, but it is clear from the text that the author is worried about alternative interpretations of Jesus, although the precise nature of this interpretation eludes us (2:22–23; 4:2–3). The countermeasure in the sermon is to demarcate these teachers as outsiders that embody everything that the community is not (Roitto 2013). They are "antichrists," "not from us," "liars," "deniers," "deceivers" and "false prophets," inspired by "the spirit of error" (2:18–26; 4:1–6). In social identity theory, this is called the meta-contrast principle: groups tend to formulate their social identity so that the distinctiveness toward relevant outgroups become as clear as possible (Oakes 1990). As previously discussed, we must suspect that the sermon is not just describing an existing social and doctrinal divide but is trying to create one in the midst of a fuzzy social situation where the recipient assemblies still have contact with both the Johannine School and the group that the sermon opposes. The sermon aims to pull the assemblies closer to the Johannine School and farther away from the Schismatic School. In terms of network theory: The sermon aims to strengthen the weak ties to the Johannine School and eliminate the weak ties to the competitors, so as to insulate the Johannine assemblies from susceptibility to theological information channels other than themselves. Thereby, the Johannine School would achieve greater control over the Johannine social network and thereby over the formulation of Johannine Christian identity and theology (cf. Kadushin 2012: 60–61).

Concluding Summary and Discussion

Since the Johannine Community was not an isolationist sect in one location, but rather an open network of assemblies with weak translocal leadership structures, its identity and theology were bound to be contested among its participants. In this network, the Johannine School attempted to strengthen the community's identity by sending itinerant teachers and circulating letters (2–3 John), written sermons (1 John) and probably also the Gospel of John. However, they were not the only ones with a vision of the Johannine identity, so other groups in the Johannine network sent out their own teachers. Some assemblies, such as that of Diotrephes, decided to isolate themselves from the Johannine School.

By using social network analysis, we can see how the Epistles of John attempt not only to promote their vision of the community's identity and theology, but also to strengthen their own position in the Johannine social network and weaken the position of its competitors. Insistence on distance from competing teachings is central to 1 and 2 John, while 3 John is occasioned by the Johannine School being marginalized by an assembly. We do not know to what extent the Johannine School succeeded in their own time. All we know is that their texts and probably also many of their assemblies were incorporated into the larger network of Christianity in the second century. Perhaps some of the assemblies took another route, created independent social networks, and developed some of the forms of Christianity that were deemed heretic in the second century, but that, I think, is beyond our knowledge, since the Johannine letters are unreliable sources to the beliefs of its opponents.

Acknowledgement: The research for this article was funded by the Swedish Research Council, grant nr. 2016-02319.

Bibliography

Anderson, Gary A. 2009. *Sin: A History*. New Haven, CT: Yale University Press.

Ascough, Richard J. 1996. "Translocal Relationships Among Voluntary Associations and Early Christianity." *Journal of Early Christian Studies* 5: 223–241.

Ascough, Richard J. 2015. "Paul, Synagogues, and Associations: Reframing the Question of Models for Pauline Christ Groups." *Journal of the Jesus Movement in Its Jewish Setting* 2: 27–52.

Ascough, Richard J. 2015. "What are They Now Saying about Christ Groups and Associations?" *Currents in Biblical Research* 13: 207–244.

Atkinson, Quentin D. and Pierrick Bourrat. 2011. "Beliefs about God, the Afterlife and Morality Support the Role of Supernatural Policing in Human Cooperation." *Evolution and Human Behavior* 32: 41–49.

Axelrod, Robert. 1984. *The Evolution of Cooperation*. New York: Basic Books.

Axelrod, Robert. 1997. *The Complexity of Cooperation: Agent-Based Models of Competition and Collaboration*. Princeton, NJ: Princeton University Press.

Barnes, Timothy D. 1985. *Tertullian: A Historical and Literary Study*, rev. ed. Oxford: Clarendon Press.

Barrett, Justin L. and E. Thomas Lawson. 2001. "Ritual Intuitions: Cognitive Contributions to Judgments of Ritual Efficacy." *Journal of Cognition and Culture* 1: 183–201.

Bar-Tal, Daniel. 1990. *Group Beliefs: A Conception for Analyzing Group Structure, Processes, and Behavior*. Berlin: Springer.

Barton, Carlin A. 2001. *Roman Honor: The Fire in the Bones*. Berkeley, CA: University of California Press.

Bell, Catherine. 1997. *Ritual: Perspectives and Dimensions*. Oxford: Oxford University Press.

Bianchi, Ugo, and René Gothoni. 2005. "Confessions of Sins." In *Encyclopedia of Religion*, vol. 3, 2nd ed., edited by Lindsay Jones, 1883–1890. Detroit and New York: Macmillan.

Braithwaite, John, and Stephen Mugford. 1994. "Conditions of Successful Reintegration Ceremonies: Dealing with Juvenile Offenders." *British Journal of Criminology* 34: 139–171.

Braithwaite, John. 1989. *Crime, Shame and Reintegration*. Cambridge: Cambridge University Press.

Brown, Raymond E. 1979. *The Community of the Beloved Disciple: The Life, Loves and Hates of an Individual Church in a New Testament Times*. New York: Paulist Press.

Bulbulia, Joseph. 2004. "The Cognitive and Evolutionary Psychology of Religion." *Biology and Philosophy* 19: 655–686.

Carmody, Timothy R. 1989." Matt 18:15–17 in relation to three texts from Qumran Literature (CD 9:2–8, 16–22; 1QS 5:25–6:1)." In *To Touch the Text. Biblical and Related Studies in Honor of Joseph A. Fitzmyer, S.J.*, edited by Maurya P. Horgan and Paul J. Kobelski, 141–158. New York: Crossroad.

Chwe, Michael Suk-Young. 2001. *Rational Ritual: Culture, Coordination, and Common Knowledge.* Princeton, NJ: Princeton University Press.

Crook, Zeba. 2007. "Structure versus Agency in Studies of the Biblical Social World: Engaging with Louise Lawrence." *Journal for the Study of the New Testament* 29: 251–275.

Crook, Zeba. 2009. "Honor, Shame, and Social Status Revisited." *Journal of Biblical Literature* 128: 591–611.

Culpepper, R. Alan and Paul N. Anderson, eds. 2014. *Communities in Dispute: Current Scholarship on the Johannine Epistles.* Atlanta, GA: SBL Press.

Culpepper, R. Alan. 1975 *The Johannine School: An Evaluation of the Johannine-School Hypothesis Based on an Investigation of the Nature of Ancient Schools.* SBLMS 26. Missoula, MT: Scholars Press.

Czachesz, István. 2011. "Women, Charity and Mobility in Early Christianity: Weak Links and the Historical Transformation of Religions." In *Changing Minds: Religion and Cognition Through the Ages.*, edited by István Czachesz and Tamás Biró, 129–154. Leuven: Peeters.

Czachesz, István. 2017. *Cognitive Science and the New Testament: A New Approach to Early Christian Research.* Oxford: Oxford University Press.

Dallen, James. 1986. *The Reconciling Community: The Rite of Penance.* Collegeville, MN: Liturgical Press.

Davies, W. D. and Dale C. Allison. 1991. *A Critical and Exegetical Commentary on the Gospel According to Saint Matthew*, vol. 2: *Commentary on Matthew VIII-XVIII.* ICC. Edinburgh: T&T Clark.

DeMaris, Richard E. 2008. *The New Testament in Its Ritual World.* London: Routledge.

DeSilva, David A. 1996. "Worthy of His Kingdom: Honor Discourse and Social Engineering in 1 Thessalonians." *Journal for the Study of the New Testament* 64: 49–79.

DeSilva, David A. 2000a. *Perseverance in Gratitude: A Socio-Rhetorical Commentary on the Epistle 'to the Hebrews'.* Grand Rapids, MI: Eerdmans.

DeSilva, David A. 2000b. *Honor, Patronage, Kinship & Purity: Unlocking New Testament Culture.* Downers Growe, IL: Inter-Varsity.

DeSilva, David A. 2009. *Seeing Things John's Way: The Rhetoric of the Book of Revelation.* Louisville, KY: Westminster John Knox Press.

Doskocil, Walter. 1958. *Der Bann in der Urkirche: eine rechtsgeschichtliche Untersuchung.* München: Zink.

Duling, Dennis C. 2013. "Paul's Aegean Network: The Strength of Strong Ties." *Biblical Theology Bulletin* 43: 135–154.

Duling, Dennis. 1998. "Matthew 18:15–17: Conflict, Confrontation, and Conflict Resolution in a 'Fictive Kin' Association." *Biblical Theology Bulletin* 29: 4–22.

Duling, Dennis. 2011. *A Marginal Scribe: Studies in the Gospel of Matthew in a Social-Scientific Perspective.* Eugene, OR: Wipf and Stock.

Dunn, Geoffrey D. 2004. *Tertullian.* London: Routledge.

Edwards, Derek, and Jonathan Potter. 1992. *Discursive Psychology: Inquiries in Social Construction.* London: SAGE.

Elliott, John H. 2002. "Jesus Was Not an Egalitarian: A Critique of an Anachronistic and Idealist Theory." *Biblical Theology Bulletin* 32: 75–91.

Esler, Philip. F. 2005. "Social-Scientific Models in Biblical Interpretation." In *Ancient Israel: The Old Testament in Its Social Context*, edited by Philip. F. Esler, 3–14. London: SCM.

Eubank, Nathan. 2013. *Wages of Cross-bearing and Debt of Sin: The Economy of Heaven in Matthew's Gospel*. Berlin: De Gruyter.

Favazza, Joseph A. 1988. *The Order of Penitents: Historical Roots and Pastoral Future*. Collegeville, MN: Liturgical Press.

Fischer, Ronald, and Dimitris Xygalatas. 2014. "Extreme Rituals as Social Technologies." *Journal of Cognition and Culture* 14: 345–355

Fitzgerald, Allan. 2008. "Penance." In *The Oxford Handbook of Early Christian Studies,* edited by Susan Ashbrook Harvey and David G. Hunter, 786–907. Oxford: Oxford University Press.

Fitzgerald, John T. 1996. *Friendship, Flattery, and Frankness of Speech: Studies on Friendship in the New Testament World*. Leiden: Brill.

France, Richard T. 2007. *The Gospel of Matthew*. NICNT. Grand Rapids, MI: Eerdmans

Galinsky, Adam D., Gillian Ku, and Cynthia S. Wang. 2005. "Perspective-Taking and Self-Other Overlap: Fostering Social Bonds and Facilitating Social Coordination." *Group Processes & Intergroup Relations* 8: 109–124.

Gilbert, Paul. 2003. "Evolution, Social Roles, and the Differences in Shame and Guilt." *Social Research* 70: 1205–1230.

Gilmore, David D., ed. 1987. *Honor and Shame and the Unity of the Mediterranean*. Washington, DC: American Anthropological Association.

Goldhahn-Müller, Ingrid. 1989. *Die Grenze der Gemeinde: Studien zum Problem der zweiten Busse in Neuen Testament unter Berücksichtigung der Entwicklung im 2. Jh. bis Tertullian*. Göttingen: Vandenhoeck & Ruprecht.

Granovetter, Mark. 1982. "The Strength of Weak Ties: A Network Theory Revisited." *Sociological Theory* 1: 201–233.

Greenwald, Deborah. F. and David W. Harder. 1998. "Domains of Shame: Evolutionary, Cultural, and Psychotherapeutic Aspects." In *Shame: Interpersonal Behavior, Psychopathology and Culture,* edited by Paul Gilbert and Bernice Andrews, 225–245. New York: Oxford University Press.

Gundry, Robert H. 1994. *Matthew: A Commentary on His Handbook for a Mixed Church Under Persecution*. 2. ed. Grand Rapids, MI: Eerdmans.

Hakola, Raimo. 2015. *Reconsidering Johannine Christianity: A Social Identity Approach*. New York: Routledge.

Hallonsten, Gösta. 1982. "Some aspects on the so-called 'Verdienstbegriff' of Tertullian." In *Studia patristica: Papers Presented at the Eighth International Conference on Patristic Studies met in Oxford from 3 to 8 September 1979,* edited by Elizabeth A. Livingstone, 799–802. Elkins Park, PA: Franklin Book.

Hallonsten, Gösta. 1984. *Satisfactio bei Tertullian: Überprüfung einer Forschungstradition*. Studia Theologica Lundensia 39. Malmö: LiberFörlag/Gleerup.

Hammond, Ross A. and Robert Axelrod. 2006. "The Evolution of Ethnocentrism." *Journal of Conflict Resolution* 50: 926–936.

Harland, Philip A. 2009. *Dynamics of Identity in the World of the Early Christians: Associations, Judeans, and Cultural Minorities*. New York: T & T Clark.

Harland, Philip A. n.d. "Associations in the Greco-Roman World: An Expanding Collection of Inscriptions, Papyri and Other Sources," http://philipharland.com/greco-roman-associations/ .

Hempel, Charlotte. 1997. "The Penal Code Reconsidered." In *Legal Texts and Legal Issues: Proceedings of the Second Meeting of the International Organization for Qumran Studies, Cambridge 1995*, edited by Moshe Bernstein, Florentino García Martínez and John Kampen, 337–348. Leiden: Brill.

Hempel, Charlotte. 1998. *The Laws of the Damascus Document: Sources, Traditions, and Redaction*. Leiden: Brill.

Hendrich, Joseph. 2009. "The Evolution of Costly Displays, Cooperation and Religion: Credibility Enhancing Displays and Their Implications for Cultural Evolution." *Evolution and Human Behavior* 30: 244–260.

Hiers, Richard H. 1985. "'Binding' and 'Loosing': The Matthean Authorizations." *Journal of Biblical Literature* 104: 233–250.

Honko, Lauri. 1979. "Theories Concerning the Ritual Process: An Orientation." In *Science of Religion: Studies in Methodology*, edited by Lauri Honko, 369–390.

Iannaccone, Laurence R. 1994. "Why Strict Churches are Strong." *American Journal of Sociology* 99: 1180–1211.

Irons, William. 1996. "Morality, Religion, and Human Nature." In *Religion and Science: History, Method, and Dialogue*, edited by W. Mark Richardson and Wesley J. Wildman, 375–399. New York: Routledge.

Irons, William. 2001. "Religion as a Hard-to-Fake Sign of Commitment." In *Evolution and the Capacity for Commitment*, edited by Randolph M. Nesse, 292–309. New York: Russell Sage Foundation.

Jaffe, Klaus. 2008. "Evolution of Shame as an Adaptation to Social Punishment and its Contribution to Social Cohesiveness." *Complexity* 14: 46–52.

Johnson, Dominic, and Jesse Bering. 2009. "Hand of God, Mind of Man: Punishment and Cognition in the Evolution of Cooperation." In *The Believing Primate: Scientific, Philosophical, and Theological Reflections on the Origin of Religion*, edited by Jeffrey Schloss and Michael Murray, 26–43. Oxford: Oxford University Press.

Johnson, Dominic, and Oliver Krüger. 2004. "The Good of Wrath: Supernatural Punishment and the Evolution of Cooperation." *Political Theology* 5: 159–176.

Johnson, Marguerite, and Terry Ryan. 2005. *Sexuality in Greek and Roman Society and Literature: A Sourcebook*. London: Routledge.

Johnson, Maxwell E. 2007. *The Rites of Christian Initiation: Their Evolution and Interpretation*. 2nd rev. and expanded ed. Collegeville, MN: Liturgical Press.

Jokiranta, Jutta. 2007. "Social Identity in the Qumran Movement: The Case of the Penal Code." In *Explaining Christian Origins and Early Judaism: Contributions from Cognitive and Social Science,* edited by Petri Luomanen, Illka Pyysiäinen, and Risto Uro, 277–298. Leiden: Brill.

Kadushin, Charles. 2014 *Understanding Social Networks: Theories, Concepts, and Findings*. Oxford: Oxford University Press.

Kampen, John. 1998. "Communal Discipline in the Social World of the Matthean Community." In *Communal Life in the Early Church: Essays Honoring Graydon F. Snyder*, edited by Julian V. Hills, 158–174. Harrisburg: Trinity Press.

Karkowski, Annerose. 2004. *Konfliktmanagement im Matthäusevangelium: Destruktive und konstruktive Gruppendynamik in der Gemeinde*. Dissertation. Neuendettelsau. [http://www.augustana.de/dokumente/promotionen/huettenmueller_konfliktmanagement.pdf]

Keener, Craig S. 1999. *A Commentary on the Gospel of Matthew.* Grand Rapids, MI: Eerdmans.

Ketola, Kimmo. 2007. "A Cognitive Approach to Ritual Systems." In *Explaining Christian Origins and Early Judaism*, edited by Petri Luomanen Ilkka Pyysiäinen, and Risto Uro, 95–114. Leiden: Brill.

Kim, Jae-Woo. 2010. "A Tag-Based Evolutionary Prisoner's Dilemma Game on Networks with Different Topologies." *Journal of Artificial Societies and Social Simulation* 13: 2.

Kloppenborg, John S. 1996. "Collegia and Thiasoi: Issues in Function, Taxonomy and Membership." In *Voluntary Associations in the Graeco-Roman World*, edited by John S. Kloppenborg and Stephen G. Wilson, 16–30. London: Routledge.

Konstan, David. 2010. *Before Forgiveness: The Origins of a Moral Idea.* Cambridge: Cambridge University Press.

Kreinath, Jens, Jan Snoek and Michael Stausberg, editors. 2008. *Theorizing Rituals: Issues, Topics, Approaches, Concepts.* Leiden: Brill.

Kugel, James L. 1987. "On Hidden Hatred and Open Reproach: Early Exegesis of Leviticus 19:17." *Harvard Theological Review* 80: 43–61.

Lakoff, George, and Mark Johnson. 1980. *Metaphors We Live by.* Chicago, IL: University of Chicago Press.

Lakoff, George, and Mark Johnson. 1999. *Philosophy in the Flesh: The Embodied Mind and Its Challenge to Western Thought.* New York: Basic Books.

Lam, Joseph. 2016. *Patterns of Sin in the Hebrew Bible: Metaphor, Culture, and the Making of a Religious Concept.* New York: Oxford University Press.

Lamb, David A. 2014. *Text, Context and the Johannine Community: A Sociolinguistic Analysis of the Johannine Writings.* New York: T&T Clark.

Lawrence, Louise J. 2002 "'For Truly, I Tell You, They Have Received Their Reward' (Matt 6:2): Investigating Honor Precedence and Honor Virtue." *Catholic Biblical Quarterly* 64: 687–702.

Lawrence, Louise J. 2003. *An Ethnography of the Gospel of Matthew: A Critical Assessment of the Use of the Honour and Shame Model in New Testament Studies.* WUNT 2.165. Tübingen: Mohr Siebeck.

Lawson, Thomas. E. and Robert. N. McCauley 1990. *Rethinking Religion: Connecting Cognition and Culture.* Cambridge: Cambridge University Press.

Le Saint, William P., transl. 1959. Tertullian, *Treatises on Penance.* Westminster: Newman.

Lieu, Judith. 2008. "Us or You? Persuasion and Identity in 1 John." *Journal of Biblical Literature* 127: 805–819.

Lieu, Judith. 2014. "The Audience of the Johannine Epistles." In *Communities in Dispute: Current Scholarship on the Johannine Epistles*, edited by R. Alan Culpepper and Paul N. Anderson, 123–140. Atlanta, GA: SBL Press.

Lieu, Judith. *The Theology of the Johannine Epistles.* NT Theology. Cambridge: Cambridge University Press, 1991.

Luz, Ulrich. 2001. *Matthew 8–20: A Commentary.* Hermeneia. Minneapolis, MN: Fortress.

Malina, Bruce J. 1981. *The New Testament World: Insights from Cultural Anthropology.* Atlanta, GA: John Knox Press.

Malina, Bruce J. 2001. *The New Testament World: Insights from Cultural Anthropology*, 3rd revised and expanded ed. Louisville, KY: Westminster John Knox Press.

Malina, Bruce J. and Richard L. Rohrbaugh. 1998a. *Social-science Commentary on the Synoptic Gospels.* Minneapolis, MN: Fortress Press.

Malina, Bruce J. and Richard L. Rohrbaugh. 1998b. *Social-science Commentary on the Gospel of John*. Minneapolis, MN: Fortress Press.

Marques, Jose M., Dominic Abrams, and R. G. Seredio. 2001. "Being Better by Being Right: Subjective Group Dynamics and Derogation of Ingroup Deviants When Generic Norms Are Undermined." *Journal of Personality and Social Psychology* 81: 436–447.

Martyn, J. Louis. 1968. *History and Theology in the Fourth Gospel*. New York: Harper & Row.

McCauley, Robert. N. and Thomas. E. Lawson. 2002. *Bringing Ritual to Mind: Psychological Foundations of Cultural Forms*. Cambridge: Cambridge University Press.

McCullough, Michael E. 2008. *Beyond Revenge: The Evolution of the Forgiveness Instinct*. San Francisco, CA: Jossey-Bass.

McNeill, John T., and Helena M. Gamer. 1938. *Medieval Handbooks of Penance*. New York: Columbia University Press.

Moxnes, Halvor. 1996. "Honor and Shame." In *The Social Sciences and New Testament Interpretation*, edited by Richard L. Rohrbaugh, 19–40. Peabody, MA: Hendrickson Publishers.

Mullet, Étienne, and Michèle Girard. 1999. "Developmental and Cognitive Points of View on Forgiveness." In *Forgiveness: Theory, Research and Practice*, edited by M. E. McCullough, K. I. Pargament, and C. E. Thoresen, 111–132. New York: Guilford Press.

Murray, Michael J. and Lyn Moore. 2009. "Costly Signaling and the Origin of Religion." *Journal of Cognition and Culture* 9: 225–245.

Neufeld, Dietmar. 2010. "Honor: Core Value in the Biblical World." In *Understanding the Social World of the New Testament*, edited by Dietmar Neufeld and Richard E. DeMaris, 109–125. London: Routledge.

Neufeld, Dietmar. *Reconceiving Texts as Speech Acts: An Analysis of I John*. Leiden: Brill, 1994.

Neyrey, Jerome H. 1998. *Honor and Shame in the Gospel of Matthew*. Louisville, KY: Westminster John Knox Press.

Neyrey, Jerome H. 2007. *The Gospel of John*. Cambridge: Cambridge University Press.

Oakes, Penelope J. 1990. "The Categorization Process: Cognition of the Group in the Social Psychology of Stereotyping." In *Social Identity Theory: Constructive and Critical Advances.*, edited by Dominic Abrams and Michael A. Hogg, 28–47. London: Harvester Wheatsheaf.

Ohtsubo, Yohsuke and Esuka Watanabe. 2009. "Do Sincere Apologies Need to be Costly? Test of a Costly Signaling Model of Apology." *Evolution and Human Behavior* 30: 114–123.

Paden, William E. 2016. *New Patterns for Comparative Religion: Passages to an Evolutionary Perspective*. London and New York: Bloomsbury.

Painter, John. 2002. *1, 2, and 3 John*. Sacra Pagina. Collegeville, MN: Liturgical Press.

Panksepp, Jaak. 1998. *Affective Neuroscience: The Foundations of Human and Animal Emotions*. New York: Oxford University Press.

Peristiany, John George, ed. 1966. *Honour and Shame: The Values of Mediterranean Society*. London: Weidenfeld and Nicholson.

Pilch, John J. 2011. "Honor and Shame Bibliography (in progress)." http://www9.georgetown.edu/faculty/pilchj/honor.bib.html. Access date: 1 June 2022.

Pilch, John J. 2012. "Oxford Bibliographies: Honor and Shame." http://www.oxfordbibliographies.com/view/document/obo-9780195393361/obo-9780195393361-0077.xml. Access date: 1 June 2022.

Poschmann, Bernhard. 1940. *Paenitentia secunda: Die kirchliche Buße im ältesten Christentum bis Cyprian und Origenes*. Bonn: Peter Hanstein.

Rahner, Karl. 1983. *Theological Investigations,* vol. 15: *Penance in the Early Church.* New York: Crossroad.

Rankin, David. 1995. *Tertullian and the Church.* Cambridge: Cambridge University Press.

Rappaport, Roy A. 1999. *Ritual and Religion in the Making of Humanity.* Cambridge: Cambridge University Press.

Rohrbaugh, Richard L. 2010. "Honor: Core Value in the Biblical World." In *Understanding the Social World of the New Testament,* edited by Dietmar Neufeld and Richard E. DeMaris, 109–125. London: Routledge.

Roitto, Rikard. 2011. *Behaving as a Christ-Believer: A Cognitive Perspective on Identity and Behavior Norms in Ephesians.* ConBNT. Winona Lake, IN: Eisenbrauns.

Roitto, Rikard. 2012. "Practices of Confession, Intercession and Forgiveness in 1 John 1.9; 5.16." *New Testament Studies* 58: 232–253.

Roitto, Rikard. 2013. "Sinless Sinners who Remain in Him: Social Identity in 1 John." In *The T&T Clark Handbook to Social Identity and the New Testament,* edited by Brian Tucker and Coleman Baker, 493–510. London: T&T Clark, 2013.

Roitto, Rikard. 2014. "Reintegrative Shaming and a Prayer Ritual of Reintegration in Matthew 18:15–20." *Svensk Exegetisk Årsbok* 97: 95–123.

Roitto, Rikard. 2015. "The Polyvalence of ἀφίημι and the Two Cognitive Frames of Forgiveness in the Synoptic Gospels." *Novum Testamentum* 57: 136–158.

Runesson, Anders. 2013. "Purity, Holiness, and the Kingdom of Heaven in Matthew's Narrative World." In *Purity and Holiness in Judaism and Christianity: Essays in Memory of Susan Haber,* edited by Carl Ehrlich, Anders Runesson and Eileen Schuller, 144–180. WUNT 305. Tübingen: Mohr Siebeck.

Scheidel, Walter. 2011. "Monogamy and Polygyny." In *A Companion to Families in the Greek and Roman Worlds,* edited by Beryl Rawson, 108–115. Malden, MA and Oxford: Wiley-Blackwell.

Schjødt, Jens Peter. 1986. "Initiation and the Classification of Rituals." *Temenos* 22: 93–108.

Schloss, Jeffrey P. and Michael J. Murray. 2011. "Evolutionary Accounts of Belief in Supernatural Punishment: A Critical Review." *Religion, Brain and Behavior* 1: 46–99.

Slone, D. Jason, and James A. Van Slyke, eds. 2015. *The Attraction of Religion: A New Evolutionary Psychology of Religion.* London: Bloomsbury Academic.

Slone, D. Jason. 2008. "The Attraction of Religion: A Sexual Selectionist Account." In *The Evolution of Religion: Studies, Theories, & Critiques,* edited by Joseph Bulbulia et al., 181–188. Santa Margarita, CA: Collins Foundation Press.

Smalley, Stephen S. 1984. *1, 2, 3 John.* Word Biblical Commentary. Waco, TX: Word Books.

Smith, David Raymond. 2009. *Hand This Man Over to Satan: Curse, Exclusion, and Salvation in 1 Corinthians 5.* London: T&T Clark.

Sørensen, Jesper, Pierre Lienard, and Chelsea Feeny. 2006. "Agent and Instrument in Judgements of Ritual Efficacy." *Journal of Cognition and Culture* 6: 463–482.

Sosis, Richard. 2003. "Why Aren't We All Hutterites? Costly Signaling Theory and Religious Behavior." *Human Nature* 14: 91–127.

Sosis, Richard. 2004. "The Adaptive Value of Religious Ritual: Rituals Promote Group Cohesion by Requiring Members to Engage in Behavior that is Too Costly to Fake." *American Scientists* 92: 166–174.

Sosis, Richard. 2006. "Religious Behaviors, Badges, and Bans: Signaling Theory and the Evolution of Religion." In *Where God and Science Meet: How Brain and Evolutionary Studies Alter Our Understanding of Religion, Volume 1: Evolution, Genes, and the Religious Brain*, edited by Patrick McNamara, 61–86. Westport, CT: Praeger.

Sosis, Richard. 2009. "The Adaptationist-Byproduct Debate on the Evolution of Religion: Five Misunderstandings of the Adaptationist Program." *Journal of Cognition and Culture* 9: 315–332.

Sperber, Dan. 1996. *Explaining Culture: A Naturalistic Approach*. Cambridge: Blackwell.

Staw, Barry M. 1976. "Knee-deep in the Big Muddy: A Study of Escalating Commitment to a Chosen Course of Action." *Organizational Behavior and Human Performance* 16: 27–44.

Streett, Daniel R. 2011. *They Went Out from Us: The Identity of the Opponents in First John*. Berlin: De Gruyter.

Sullivan, Francis Aloysius. 2001. *From Apostles to Bishops: The Development of the Episcopacy in the Early Church*. New York: Newman Press.

Takaku, Seiji, Bernard Weiner and Ken-Ichi Ohbuchi. 2001. "A Cross-Cultural Examination of the Effects of Apology and Perspective Taking on Forgiveness." *Journal of Language and Social Psychology* 20: 144–166.

Tangney, June P. 2002. "Self-Conscious Emotions: The Self as a Moral Guide." In *Self and Motivation: Emerging Psychological Perspectives*, edited by Abraham Tesser, Diederik A. Stapel, and Joanne V. Wood, 97–117. Washington, DC: American Psychological Association.

Tangney, June P. and Ronda L. Dearing. 2002. *Shame and Guilt*. New York: Guilford Press.

Teehan, John. 2010. *In the Name of God: The Evolutionary Origins of Religious Ethics and Violence*. Hoboken, NJ: Wiley-Blackwell.

Tellbe, Mikael. 2009. *Christ-Believers in Ephesus: A Textual Analysis of Early Christian Identity Formation in a Local Perspective*. WUNT 2.242. Tübingen: Mohr Siebeck.

Theissen, Gerd. 2007. *Erleben und Verhalten der ersten Christen: Eine Psychologie des Urchristentums*. Gütersloh: Gütersloher Verlags-Haus.

Thompson, William G. 1970. *Matthew's Advice to a Divided Community: Mt. 17,22–18,35*. Rome: Biblical Institute Press.

Tilborg, Sjef van. 1996. *Reading John in Ephesus*. Leiden: Brill.

Trebilco, Paul. 2004. *The Early Christians in Ephesus from Paul to Ignatius*. WUNT 166. Tübingen: Mohr Siebeck.

Uro, Risto. 2010. "Ritual and Christian Origins." In *Understanding the Social World of the New Testament*, edited by Dietmar Neufeld and Richard E. DeMaris, 220–232. London: Routledge.

Waal, Frans B. M. de. 2013. *The Bonobo and the Atheist: In Search of Humanism Among the Primates*. New York and London: W. W. Norton & Co.

Walker-Ramisch, Sandra. 1996." Graeco-Roman Voluntary Associations and the Damascus Document. A Sociological Analysis." In *Voluntary Associations in the Graeco-Roman World*, edited by John S. Kloppenborg and Stephen G. Wilson, 128–145. London: Routledge.

Wengst, Klaus. 1981. *Bedrängte Gemeinde und Verherrlichter Christus: der historische Ort des Johannesevangeliums als Schlüssel zu seiner Interpretation*. Neukirchen-Vluyn: Neukirchener Verlag.

Studia Theologica Holmiensia

ISSN: 1401-1557. *ehs.se/sth*.

1. Göran Gunner, *När tiden tar slut: Motivförskjutningar i frikyrklig apoka-lyptisk tolkning av det judiska folket och staten Israel*. 1996.

2. Runar Eldebo, *Den ensamma tron: En studie i Frank Mangs predikan*. 1997.

3. Åke Jonsson, *Skapelseteologi: En studie av teologiska motiv i Gunnar Ed-mans texter*. 1999.

4. Rune W. Dahlén, *Med bibeln som bekännelse och bekymmer: Bibel-synsfrågan i Svenska Missionsförbundet 1917–1942 med särskild hänsyn till Missionsskolan och samfundsledningen*. 1999.

5. Göran Gunner & Sia Spiliopoulou Åkermark (red.), *Mänskliga rät-tigheter: Aktuella forskningsfrågor*. 2001.

6. Valborg Lindgärde & Åke Viberg (red.), *Drabbad: Texter om kallelse och helhjärtat engagemang*. 2002.

7. Diana Amnéus & Göran Gunner (red.), *Mänskliga rättigheter: Från for-skningens frontlinjer*. 2003.

8. Elena Namli, *Och på en enda kyrka: Ortodox ekumenik i ekumenisk dialog*. 2003.

9. MarieAnne Ekedahl & Björn Wiedel (red.), *Mötet med den splittrade män-niskan: Om själavård i postmodern tid*. 2004.

10. Rune W. Dahlén & Valborg Lindgärde (red.), *En historia berättas: Om missionsförbundare*. 2004.

11. Göran Gunner & Sven Halvardson (red.), *Jag behöver rötter och vingar: Om assyrisk/syriansk identitet i Sverige*. 2005.

12. Göran Gunner & Anders Mellbourn (red.), *Mänskliga rättigheter och samhällets skyldigheter*. 2005.

13. Sven Halvardson & Göran Gunner, *Vart tar väckelsens folk vägen? En studie av frikyrkligheten i de västvärmländska kommunerna Arvika, Eda och Årjäng.* 2006.

14. Lars Ingelstam & Johnny Jonsson & Berit Åqvist (red.), *Spår av Gud: En vänbok till Valborg Lindgärde.* 2006.

15. Hans Andreasson (red.), *Liv och rörelse: Svenska Missionskyrkans historia och identitet.* 2007.

16. Åke Viberg, *Prophets in Action: An Analysis of Prophetic Symbolic Acts in the Old Testament.* 2007.

17. Rune W. Dahlén & Runar Eldebo & Owe Kennerberg, *Församling i rörelse: Om församlingsutveckling i västra Värmland.* 2008.

18. Thomas Kazen, *Issues of Impurity in Early Judaism.* 2010.

19a. Thomas Kazen, *Emotions in Biblical Law: A Cognitive Science Approach.* 2011.

19b. Sven Halvardson, *Kanske alla har rätt – eller fel: Religionsmöten och syn på andra i mångreligiösa miljöer.* 2012.

20. Kjell-Åke Nordquist (red.), *Gods and Arms: On Religion and Armed Conflict.* 2013.

22. Josef Forsling, *Composite Artistry in the Book of Numbers: A Study in Biblical Narrative Conventions.* 2013.

23a. Sune Fahlgren, *Vatten är tjockare än blod: En baptistisk kulturhistoria.* 2015.

23b. Ulla Lind, *Kallelse och gärning i Kongokyrkan CEC.* 2015.

24. Jørgen Thaarup, *Kristendommens Morgenstjerne: Konvergerende teologiske træk med baggrund i østlig tradition hos John Wesley og NFS Grundtvig.* 2015.

25. Caroline Gustavsson, *Delaktighetens kris: Gudstjänstens pedagogiska utmaning.* 2016.

27. Rune W. Dahlén & Ulf Hållmarker & Lennart Molin, *Missionsskolan Lidingö.* 2016.

28. Jørgen Thaarup, *Med venner i lys vi tale: John Wesleys og NFS Grundtvigs konvergerende teologier.* 2016

29. Hans Andreasson, *Identitet och gestaltning: Väckelseforskning i akademi och kyrka.* 2018.

30. Thomas Kazen, *Smuts, skam, status: Perspektiv på samkönad sexualitet i Bibeln och antiken.* 2018.

31. Sune Fahlgren (red.), *Uppdrag Pastor: Teologi och praktik.* 2019.

32. Sune Fahlgren (red.), *Hela livets kyrka: Pastoral teologi för vigsel, begravning och dop.* 2019.

33. Susanne Wigorts Yngvesson & Charlotte Wells (red.), *Trolösa: Speglingar av Luther i Bergman och Bergman i Luther.* 2021.

34. Thomas Kazen & Susanne Wigorts Yngvesson (red.), *Öppna vyer – lång sikt: Festskrift till Owe Kennerberg.* 2021.

35. Thomas Kazen, *Moral Infringement and Repair in Antiquity.* Supplement 1: *Emotions and Hierarchies.* 2022.

36. Rikard Roitto, *Moral Infringement and Repair in Antiquity.* Supplement 2: *Group Dynamics.* 2022.

37. Rikard Roitto, *Moral Infringement and Repair in Antiquity.* Supplement 3: *Forgiveness.* 2022.